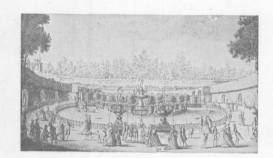

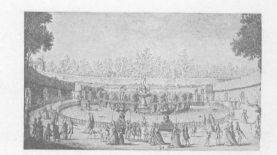

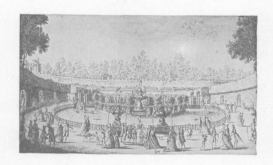

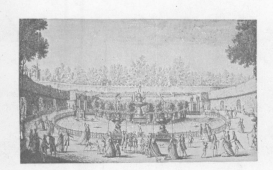
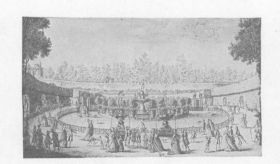
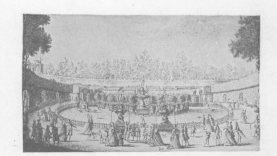

GARDENS ARE FOR PEOPLE

GARDENS

ARE FOR PEOPLE

how
to
plan
for
outdoor
living

THOMAS D. CHURCH

 REINHOLD PUBLISHING CORPORATION
New York

ACKNOWLEDGMENTS

Many of the quotations spotted throughout this book are from out-of-print works, and their inclusion, like the inclusion of quotations from books by the following publishers, is indication that we feel the books are interesting and important: John Murray, Ltd., London, for *An Essay on the Making of Gardens* by George Sitwell, 1909, on pages 3 and 79; The Macmillan Company, New York, for *An Introduction to the Study of Landscape Design* by Hubbard and Kimball, 1917, on page 4; F. W. Dodge Corporation, New York, for *Landscape for Living* by Garrett Eckbo, 1950, on page 8; P. D. and Ione Perkins, South Pasadena, for *A Thousand Years of Japanese Gardens* by Samuel Newsom, 1953, on page 22; Orange Judd Publishing Company, New York, for *The Landscape Beautiful* by Frank A. Waugh, 1910, on page 43; Studios Vie a la Campagne, Paris, for "The Garden" by Albert Maumone from *Jardins d'Aujourd'hui*, 1932, on page 94; Charles Scribner's Sons, New York, for *Gardens in the Modern Landscape* by Christopher Tunnard, 1938, on pages 120 and 174; Appleton-Century-Crofts, Inc., New York, for *Your City Garden* by Margaret McKenney and E. L. D. Seymour, 1937, on page 150; Dodd, Mead & Company, New York, for *The Story of Gardening* by Richardson Wright, 1934, on page 208.

Dedicated to Betsy, my wife, without whom . . .

GARDENS ARE FOR PEOPLE is a not a book primarily
concerned with the planting of a garden, nor does it
attempt to explain all the great underlying principles of garden
design. Many excellent books have covered these fields and
I have quoted freely from them.

It is, rather, a garden tour, with some comment in passing. It
shows what people wanted and how we helped them to
get it, or if they didn't know, how we helped them to decide.
Since the dates shown, some of the gardens have changed
hands, but we have given the name of the owners for whom
they were designed and installed.

The photographs, not otherwise credited, were taken by
the author.

If many of my remarks and most of my pictures
seem slanted toward the West Coast, you will understand that
most of my professional experience has been in California.
I can only hope that much of what is shown is universal in
its application and will vary only as it is affected by local
climates and practices.

During twenty years of garden making I have learned much from
all who have passed through the office. Of them many have
gone on to professional practices of their own—Ruth Jaffe, Marie
Berger, Douglas Baylis, Robert Royston, Theodore Osmundson
and Lawrence Halprin.

During the preparation of this book my present associates have
willingly joined in my sixteen hour day to make our dead-
line. June Meehan and Elsie Louise Sculthorp have pored over
the manuscript, correcting my English and scolding me
for my sentence construction. They have withstood my ill tem-
pers, reminded me to eat, soothed neglected clients, and
searched out the quotations which appear throughout the pages.
Casey Kawamoto is responsible for most of the drawings,
and Jack Stafford has shouldered the task of holding our practice
together in one of our busiest years.

To list the people who, directly or indirectly, have helped would
be pleasant, but endless. To invaluable friends,
co-operative clients, architects, photographers, and
magazine editors I am very grateful. Especially are we indebted
to *House Beautiful* magazine for the use of the color
plates and the Maynard Parker photographs which have appeared in their magazine during the past eight years,
and to their editors Elizabeth Gordon and Joseph Howland for
encouragement and advice during the book's preparation

Thomas D. Church
San Francisco 1955

Contents

And furthermore, my son, be admonished: of making books there is no end, and much study is a weariness of the flesh.—*Ecclesiastes, 12*

Gardens are for people

And whether doe they withdraw themselves from the troublesome affayres of their estate, being tyred with the hearing and judging of litigious Controversies, choked (as it were) with the close ayres of their sumptuous buildings, their eares filled and over-burthened with tedious discoursings. Whither? But into their Orchards? made and prepared, dressed and destinated for that purpose to renew and refresh their sences, and to call home their ever-wearied spirits. *"A New Orchard and Garden"—William Lawson, 1618*

GARDENS
are for people

Places are not to be laid out with a view to their appearance in a picture, but to their uses, and the enjoyment of them in real life; and their conformity to those purposes is that which constitutes their beauty. . . . *Rt. Hon. William Windham, in a letter to Humphrey Repton, on his controversy with Uvedale Price, 1794*

. . . a garden shal workemanly be handled and dressed unto the necessarie use and commoditie of man's life. . . . *"The Gardener's Labyrinth" —Thomas Hill, 1577*

IN ANY AGE OF REASON,
it is the owner who finally decides the size of his garden and the purposes for which it shall be used.

The garden owner is being constructive about his problems when he analyzes what he really wants as disassociated from what tradition may have convinced him he *ought* to have. Assuming he stays within the vague bounds of good taste, he *can* have just what he wants.

There are no mysterious "musts," no set rules, no finger of shame pointed at the gardener who doesn't follow an accepted pattern.

Landscaping is not a complex and difficult art to be practiced only by high priests. It is logical, down-to-earth, and aimed at making your plot of ground produce exactly what you want and need from it.

What *do* you want and need? Take a long and earnest look into your crystal ball. You will see that economic pressures have reduced the average house to a minimum and that the functions of the house have spilled over into the garden. You will see that you need additional space for lounging, eating, and entertaining; you will see that your closets and garage are bulging with a miscellany of personal belongings, tools, play equipment, *ad infinitum*, which the site must provide for.

Yet it must also perform its primary function of being a garden in the true sense of providing trees and flowers, fruits and vegetables; a place where man can recapture his affinity with the soil, if only on Saturday afternoons. It must be a green oasis where memories of his bumper-to-bumper ride from work will be erased.

To weigh, advise, interpret, integrate, and come up with some answers beyond the ability and imagination of the layman is the role of the landscape architect.

CHAPTER ONE

Introduction to design

There are a number of phrases in use which
express in general terms our longing to live *in*
our site, such as "the integration of the
house and garden," "indoor-outdoor living" and
"the relation of shelter to land."

Some years ago a garden magazine, throwing caution
to the winds, published an article called "The
Wedding of the House and Garden."

It is not a new idea. The Egyptians planned their houses
and gardens together. . . . The Romans knew all
about it. The Greeks had a word for it; and
the Renaissance Italians developed it to a fine art.
They had outside living rooms, dining rooms, corridors,
and entrance halls. They borrowed line and
materials from the house; and they borrowed foliage,
shade, fruit, flowers, and the play of water
from nature. It was a subtle compromise. The struggle
of forces—the light touch of nature and the
heavy hand of man—left no trace of incongruity.
The garden was a transitional stage saving
them from the embarrassment of stepping from
their house to nature in the raw.

The Chinese style laid its delicate hand on all the arts in
the 18th century. It influenced the English
school of landscape gardening and sent them all scurrying
back to Nature for inspiration. The waving
line was proclaimed a true line of beauty, forgetting that
a straight line is the best foil for the graceful
curves in flower and plant.

Nature was out-natured. Faked dead trees and crum-
bling ruins were added to heighten the effect
of natural decay. Lancelot ("Capability") Brown constructed a river across an estate which he considered so beautiful that he cried, "Alas! The Thames
will never forgive me!" Terraces were plowed
under, the incomparable Elizabethan flower gardens
were discovered to be unnatural. Trim Tudor
gardens with their borders of "sweet smelling herbes"
were out of style, and many of them were de-
stroyed before the wave had spent its strength.

Humphrey Repton followed a few years later, gathered
up the pieces, and, putting them together in
logical order, made nature a full partner in the humanized
landscape. But the generations of smaller home
owners in the next century, who attempted to recreate
these natural scenes on their own small plots of

After you have laid out the great walls
and chief defigns you may furnish the
rest of your garden with feveral different defigns as Tall groves, Quincunxes,
Galleries and Halls of Verdure, Labyrinths, Bowling greens and Ampithea-
tres adorned with fountains. All these
works distinguish a garden from what
is common and contribute not a little
to render it magnificent. *"The Theory
and Practice of Gardening"—Alexander LeBlond, 1728*

VILLA D'ESTE

BUTLER GARDEN, PASATIEMPO 1935

ground, were misled. Nature is not easily
transplanted to one's back yard.

This 18th century rediscovery of nature in the garden
and the 19th century vulgar adaptation of its
principles became our immediate heritage. Naturalness,
as a state of mind, is highly desirable, but to
follow blindly the frank conventions of "informal"
gardening is no guarantee that you'll get it.

We're all different; and our gardens and what we expect
our land to do for us will vary as much as our
demands and our personalities. No one can design
intelligently for you unless he knows what you need, what
you want, and what you are like. If you
won't tell, he will have to guess.

Walter L. Doty of *Sunset* magazine says, "It's just as
wrong to give an owner who is not an ambitious
gardener a combination of natural plantings requiring
expert knowledge and care as it is to give a real
'green thumb' gardener a garden with no soil to dig in."

The direction in which to move will be determined by
the desires of the people who expect to find
happiness in their gardens. Happiness will come by adding
as much beauty and by eliminating as many
irritations as possible within the limits of the problem.
The limits of the problem will be the restrictions
and opportunities of the site and the ability of the owner
and designer to overcome or make use of them.

. . . "You can't hope to persuade us
that Nature built the house, why insult our understanding by pretending
that Nature made the Garden?". . . .
It may be argued further that real
beauty is neither in garden nor landscape, but in the relation of both to the
individual, that what we are seeking is
not only a scenic setting for pool and
fountain and parterre, but a background for life. *"On the Making of
Gardens"—Sir George Sitwell, 1909*

The great challenge for the garden designer is not to make the garden look
natural, but to make the garden so the
people in it will feel natural. *Lawrence
Halprin in a letter to* House Beautiful,
May 1948

People affect the design

THE OWNER WHO IS TO USE AND PAY FOR THE GARDEN MUST BE HEARD. ANY TENDENCY TO DESIGN FOR DESIGN'S SAKE, TO CREATE A PATTERN WITHIN WHICH THE OWNER MUST LIVE ACCORDING TO RULES SET BY THE DESIGNER, IS HEADED FOR FRUSTRATION, IF NOT DISASTER.

The landscape architect should remember that he is seldom called in primarily to express his own ideas, but rather to interpret and express the client's half-formed desires. . . . *"The Introduction to the Study of Landscape Design" —Hubbard and Kimball, 1917*

So let us look closely at the owner and try to understand how he influences the design and why, within the limits of reason, and occasionally without the limits of reason, he should have what he wants.

He is influenced by the necessity of making a background for himself and his family. He is intent upon raising his standard of living. He is torn by violent whims and saddled with fascinating hobbies which should find expression in his planning.

He is often embarrassed by a real desire for beauty, and is constantly amazed by the mysteries of nature. ("I planted some seeds and they CAME UP!")

He accepts the materials and methods of modern technology as a matter of course.

He may be mainly interested in a garden in which to sit, eat, sleep, and contemplate nature in carefree surroundings.

Or he may begrudge every square foot that can't be used for intensive gardening.

He may collect odd animals and birds or be an expert on the cross-pollenization of bearded iris.

He may live in town or in the suburbs, on a ranch or in a vineyard, but he's interested in developing his land to its fullest.

The Kent Leavitts in Milbrook have a dairy and want their brown Swiss in their landscape. (Animals, birds, butterflies, and bees lend interest, color, and movement to any scene.)

HENCE IT BEHOOVES THE DESIGNER TO LISTEN AND OBSERVE BEFORE GETTING ANY PRECONCEIVED NOTIONS ABOUT HOW HIS CLIENT'S GARDEN SHOULD BE ARRANGED.

My beloved is gone down into his garden, to the beds of spices, to feed in the gardens, and to gather lilies. *"Song of Solomon"*

Consider the Peter Breinigs, who planned a small house in a hillside orchard. Sunny perennial borders immediately came to mind, with perhaps knotted boxwood gardens and roses running riot. But the Breinigs were not gardeners.

They were interested only in cooking and wished to spend their spare time among their recipes. They wanted herbs, vegetables, and berries and a space outside for preparing them, with a small terrace for tasting.

Some ornamentals crept in, but it's really a garden for a cook.

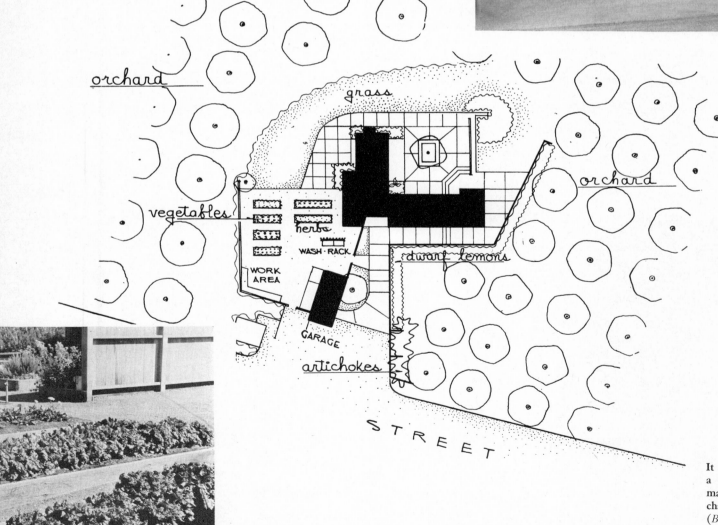

orchard

grass

orchard

vegetables

herbs

WASH·RACK

WORK AREA

dwarf lemons

GARAGE

artichokes

STREET

It is a commodious and a pleasant thing in a mansion to have an orchard of sundry fruytes. (*Borde*) *"Gleanings from Old Garden Literature"—Hazlitt, 1887*

MR. & MRS. PETER BREINIG, LOS ALTOS 1949

ARCHITECTS: WURSTER, BERNARDI & EMMONS   PHOTOGRAPHER: ROGER STURTEVANT

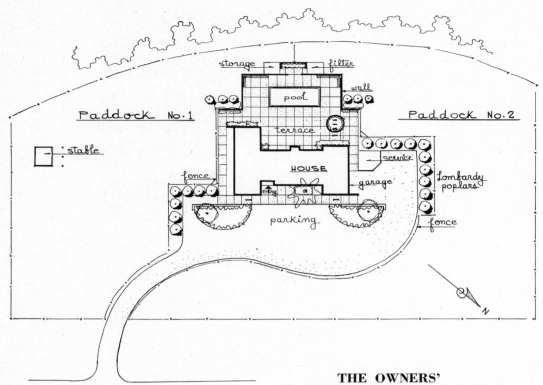

THE OWNERS' HOBBIES DETERMINED THIS GARDEN PLAN

THE HOUSE

THE EDWARDSES RELAX

Here is a new house on a flat acre of land. It's well oriented, with a pleasant background of trees. The house has progressed to the stage when landscaping should begin in earnest. There are many interesting possibilities—but who will move in? What will be their requirements, their inexplicable vagaries, their conceits? Will they garden only on weekends? Will they feel deeply emotional about everything that grows— and want it? Will they want privacy, or wide open spaces?

They could want a large flowing lawn—or refuse to cut any grass at all. They could specialize in rare Hemerocallis or want only the simplest natives. They could entertain lavishly and need a terrace for a hundred guests, or they might consider eight people a mob.

But come to find out, the Don Edwards moved to the country for two things—swimming and horses (neither of which they had been able to have in their apartment). Their landscape is a concrete terrace, two paddocks and a swimming pool. There are some trees to shade the horses and a few geraniums for color.

They'll never smell freshly cut turf or know the joys of dividing perennials, but they'll have piles of manure to give to friends. They'll ride and swim and lean over the corral fence with a lump of sugar. Occasionally someone will have to cook, and pick the dead flowers off the geraniums, but that's easy when you've got what you want.

You wouldn't like the flies, odors, noises? But you see, you're different. It doesn't matter to someone who loves horses.

MR. & MRS. DON EDWARDS, WOODSIDE 1954

ARCHITECTS: JONES & EMMONS   LANDSCAPE CONTRACTOR: OUTDOOR CONSTRUCTION, INC.

The pool, the terrace, and the horse

Mr. Edwards' arm is in a cast, but he
didn't break it pulling weeds. He
fell off his horse.

If these examples are exceptions—what then,
does the average man think about his surroundings?
What changes have taken place, socially
and economically, that make his garden differ
from those of a generation ago?

He, his wife and his children, realize it's
a changing world and like it.

Things *have* changed.

The large lot with a stable has changed to a small
lot with a garage absorbed into the house.

The change from tea in the parlor to drinks in the garden gives
us the terrace or outside room, which increases in
importance as the house gets smaller.

The change from high-neck ruffles and bloomers to
the Bikini gives us the sun-bathing terrace.

The change from long lace dresses and perambulators to infant
nakedness gives us the modern child's play yard.

The automobile has changed our entrance from a
circular carriage driveway to a parking lot.

Lack of gardeners has given us the owner's service area complete with potting bench, mulch bin, and a lath house.

Gunite and plastic swimming pools bring this former luxury
tantalizingly within our reach.
The nurseries are filled with plants and trees from all over the
world and the seed catalogs offer a blinding array of color.

We are given every help and cure-all that American ingenuity can
think of, from soil conditioners that will turn clay into
leafmold overnight to sprays that will eliminate all pests and
fertilize the garden as well. We try them all and
shrug it off if they won't work.

The average home owner today wants to use his garden to
work in, to play in, and to relax in; he's proud of it.

Busse, Los Angeles—
Cliff May, Designer

A terrace
A tree
A lanai
A small lawn
Native shrubs
Sun, shade and
privacy

ANIMALS BELONG IN THE LANDSCAPE

If plants are the primary framework of a garden, animals are one of its major enrichments. *"Landscape for Living"—Garrett Eckbo, 1950*

THE VINEYARD IS THEIR LANDSCAPE

MR. & MRS. ERNEST GALLO, MODESTO 1941   ARCHITECT: GARDNER A. DAILEY   PHOTOGRAPHER: PHILIP FEIN

The site affects design

(and site improvements affect the budget)

GOOD PROPERTY IS NO LONGER EASY TO FIND.

The perfect site is on slightly rising ground with large healthy trees, a fine view, or a beautiful background of foliage; it has deep, rich topsoil and is oriented to be out of the wind— but to catch all the sunshine. As long as we're dreaming, we might as well add that it is near schools, churches and shops and that all utilities are already at the property line. If you find it, buy it.

IF YOU'RE GOING TO LOOK FOR PROPERTY, take your architect and landscape architect along—they are qualified to advise you. The real estate agent is not trained to tell you if it's a suitable site for you. His business is to sell it. The landscape architect can measure your requirements and your budget against the probable cost of developing the property. Maybe the trees are either poor varieties or in bad condition; maybe it's covered with obnoxious weeds which would be almost impossible to eradicate. There may be grading problems that aren't obvious. There may be indications of poor drainage, heavy clay soil, erosion or exposure that should influence your decision. If you're looking at the property on a hot summer day and find it lush and cool, you may forget it's a north slope with no sun from October to March.

MOST PEOPLE START OUT WITH A BUDGET. The only way to hope to stay within it is to avoid as much guesswork as you can and to know all possible costs before you commit yourself. To the average layman the headings are simple: the lot, the house, the furniture, the garden (it will be done gradually later). The garden allowance covers only soil preparation, plants, and lawns.

BUT—EVER HEAR OF SITE IMPROVEMENTS? They're seldom included in the first budget and yet they are real costs. Aside from special conditions imposed by the site or the client's whims they consist of tree clearing and rough grading, boundary fences, entrance road and parking, additional leveling and fine grading after the house is built, retaining walls, drainage system, hose bibbs and sprinklers, garden structures (tool house, bath house, extra storage), screen fences within the garden and garden lighting. Most of them should be done before you move in. On a simple, flat lot they may not strain your budget, but on tough terrain they may cost as much as the house itself.

Don't cross your fingers and hope the bids will come in low. They won't. The things you will have to eliminate may be the things you want most.

FIND OUT WHERE YOU'RE GOING BEFORE YOU START.

A man who would plant a handſome garden ſhoud do two things: Make Choice of a perſon of very good ability in the Art of Gardening; and he be well adviſed about the Charge, that the ſize of his Building and the extent of his garden may be anſwerable to the Expence he would be at. *"Theory and Practice of Gardening"—John James, 1712*

We start ". . . with the idea that our land will cost but $6000, and our house $8000, and our stable $1000, and sundries $500. But unfortunately, these sundries are the rocks on which much rural enthusiasm is lost. It is the ice-house, and the root-house, and the gardener's house, and the green-house, and the grape-house, with the grading, and road making, and trenching, and digging, and the labor necessary to keep these all up, that exhaust both our enthusiasm and our purse. . . ." *Supplement by Henry Winthrop Sargent to "Landscape Gardening"—A. J. Downing, 1859*

MR. & MRS. DEWEY DONNELL, SONOMA 1948

PHOTOGRAPHER: RONDAL PARTRIDGE

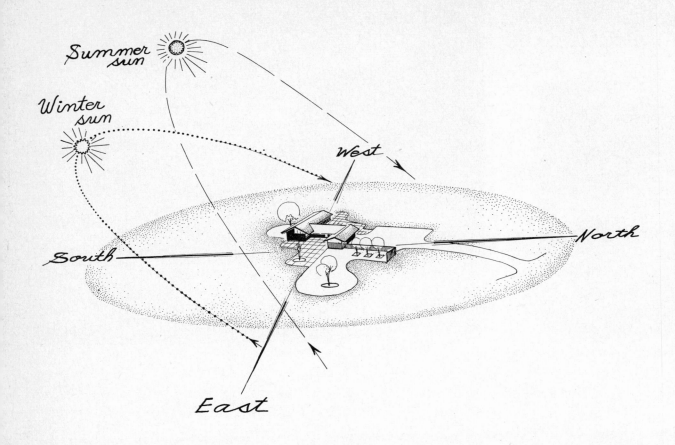

South — West — North — East — Summer sun — Winter sun

. . . above all, it should be healthful, not situate in a low or marshy ground, because of the Corruption caused there by the infectious Breath of Venomous Animals which breed there and occasion many Noxious Humours and Distempers; and that the House be not turned to the South or West, because Heat weakens the Body and Cold strengthens it.—*Vitruvius*

ORIENTATION *SHOULD* AFFECT DESIGN.

Look carefully at your site before you sigh and place the house square to the property lines with the living room on the street and the kitchen and garage at the rear. Rooms can go anywhere you want them for the right amount of sun at the right time of year. Wings of the house can protect garden areas. If you want large areas of glass, be wary of south and west exposures. No amount of overhang will shield the glass from the late summer sun. Your pleasure will be diminished if you have to close heavy drapes at four o'clock.

Since we can't all have the famous house which turns with the seasons, get the best possible orientation for the house and the garden areas.

▶

**TOPOGRAPHY
AFFECTS
DESIGN**

THE SITE FORCED THIS GARDEN
ALONG A NARROW RIDGE

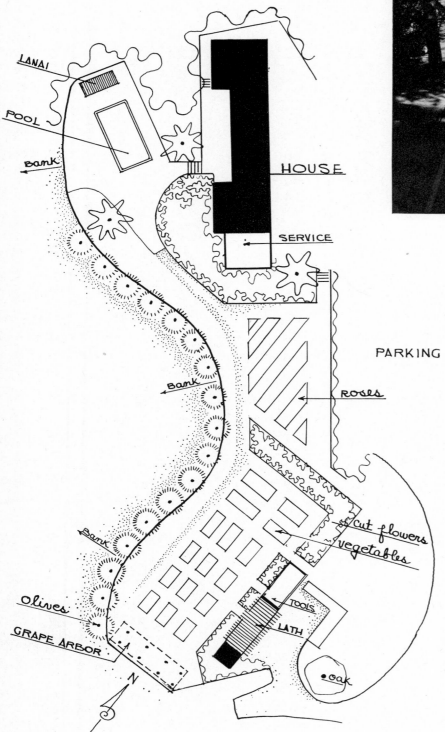

The Sullivan place in the country lies
along the top of a rocky ridge with fine
views in all directions.

The amenities they wanted—a pool, roses, fruit
trees and vegetables—are strung out
along the only level area.

The rose garden and vegetable beds are raised,
not only for neatness and convenience,
but because they are built on a rock base. It
proved to be a much more economical
way to get sufficient topsoil than to excavate and
drain the garden planting space.

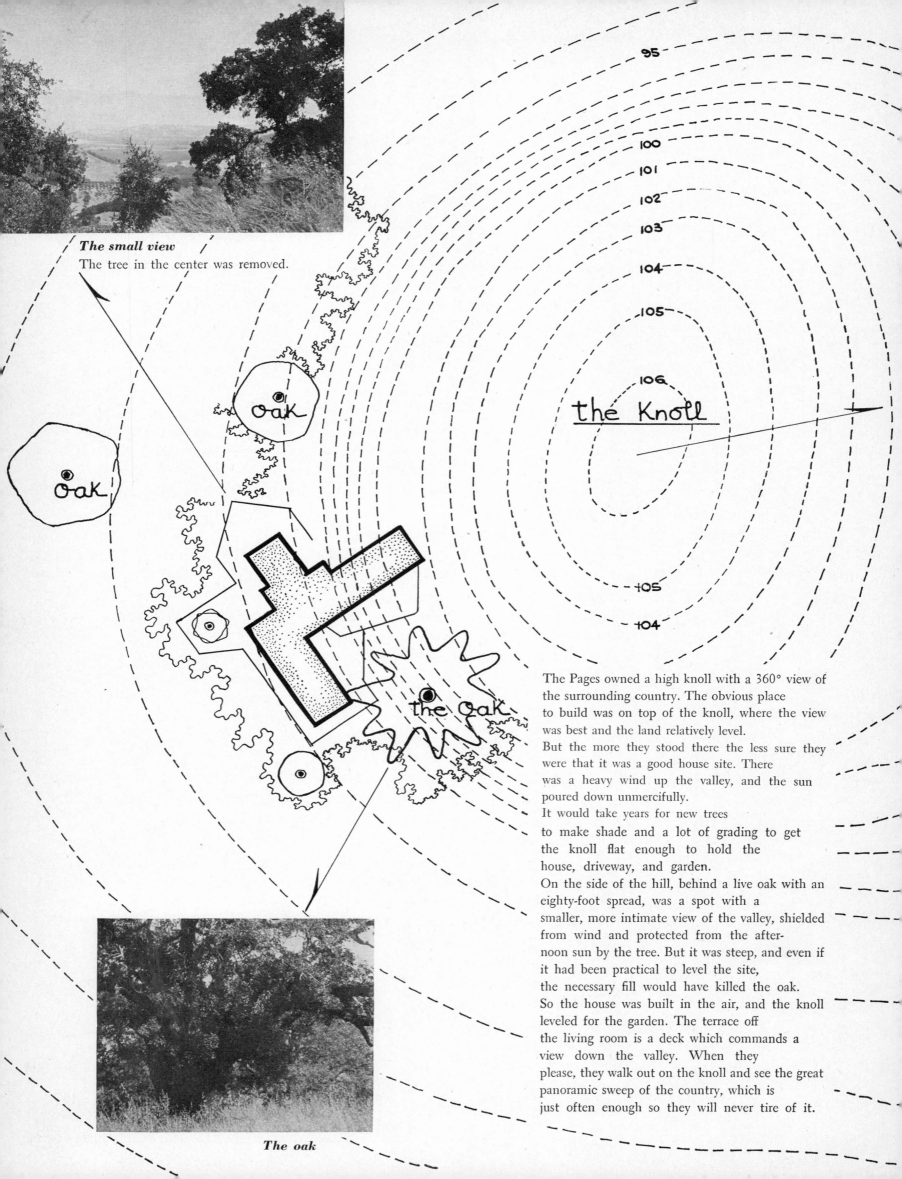

The small view
The tree in the center was removed.

95
100
101
102
103
104
105
106

the Knoll

105
104

the Oak

The Pages owned a high knoll with a 360° view of
the surrounding country. The obvious place
to build was on top of the knoll, where the view
was best and the land relatively level.
But the more they stood there the less sure they
were that it was a good house site. There
was a heavy wind up the valley, and the sun
poured down unmercifully.
It would take years for new trees
to make shade and a lot of grading to get
the knoll flat enough to hold the
house, driveway, and garden.
On the side of the hill, behind a live oak with an
eighty-foot spread, was a spot with a
smaller, more intimate view of the valley, shielded
from wind and protected from the afternoon sun by the tree. But it was steep, and even if
it had been practical to level the site,
the necessary fill would have killed the oak.
So the house was built in the air, and the knoll
leveled for the garden. The terrace off
the living room is a deck which commands a
view down the valley. When they
please, they walk out on the knoll and see the great
panoramic sweep of the country, which is
just often enough so they will never tire of it.

Oak
Oak

The oak

The big view

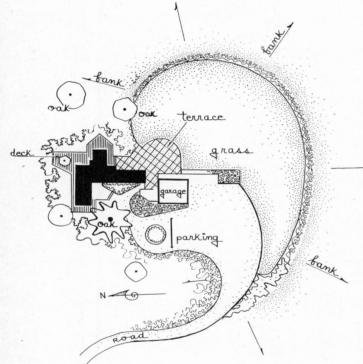

PLACING THE HOUSE

The most obvious place to put the house is not always
the right one. If there is only a small area of flat
land, you'll be tempted to use it for the house. It probably
should be saved for arrival, parking or garden.
Houses can be built on a slope, but it means a lot of
grading and walls later when you try to get
enough flat land for the areas you need around the house.

Is there one particular spot on the property that seems
just right in every way? Have you picnicked there
and found it idyllic? Have you spent long winter evenings
planning a house there? Has it occurred to you that
if you built your house there the spot will be gone? Maybe
that's where your garden should be.

Ask yourself these questions:

Do you want morning light in the bedrooms?
In a hot climate, do you like a north kitchen?
If the dominant view is to the west—and you want
the main rooms to have that view—what are
you doing about controlling the afternoon sunshine?
Is the house placed to allow adequate
arrival and parking space?
Do you know the minimum turning
radius for your car?
Can you turn in and out of your garage
without breaking your elbows?
Are the service areas large enough for all your needs?

These and many other special problems
need to be recognized and solved in a prelimi-
nary way before you go ahead.

MR. & MRS. HENRY C. PAGE, LOS GATOS 1954

Children influence design

There's no problem in planning a children's garden or playground if it's off somewhere and it doesn't matter what they do with it.

But no matter how big it is, it's amazing how often they'll be on *your* terrace. If you're planning to raise a big family, think about designing the whole space for the children *and* for you.

Normally you design your garden as you want it and give the children the balance. Reverse the process; arrange the space for their activities and put the garden in what is left. Nothing is given up —its just planned differently.

You, the children, and the delphiniums will all be happier.

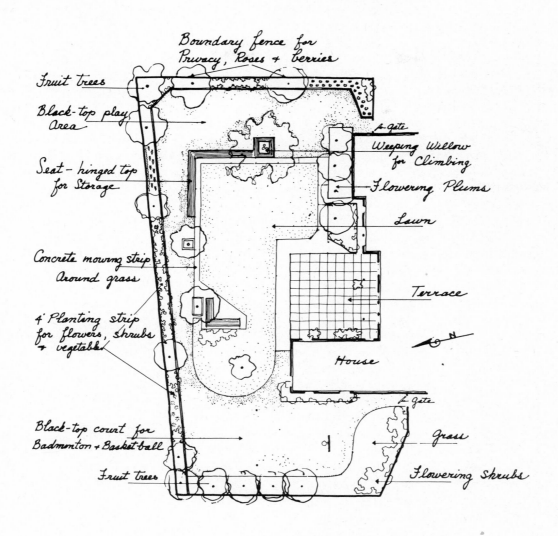

Boundary fence for
Privacy, Roses + berries

Fruit trees

Black-top play
Area

Seat - hinged top
for Storage

Concrete mowing strip
Around grass

4' Planting strip
for flowers, shrubs
+ vegetables

Black-top court for
Badminton + Basket-ball

Fruit trees

Weeping Willow
for Climbing

Flowering Plums

Lawn

Terrace

House

N

gate

gate

grass

Flowering Shrubs

A COLLABORATION BETWEEN THE GARDEN AND THE PLAYGROUND

The garden the Littlefields wanted and the play space they needed got together to make a pleasant garden for both adults and children.

In doing so, it produced all the amenities they expected when they moved to the country.

The children are given all the perimeter areas without question. The play and game areas, plus the wide path connecting them, are in blacktop. They become an obstacle course for all varieties of rolling stock. You may be the obstacle as they cross the terrace, but you can learn to dodge. There are no bad corners and no dead-ends. The children go round and round.

The garden is a four-foot wide strip around the property fence. It is raised above the blacktop with a 6" curb to keep tricycles under control. It can hold all the flowers, flowering shrubs, vegetables, and fruit trees that the average gardener could want.

The lawn is an island. It contains several trees and its own small terrace.

The area of the back yard averages about 52 feet by 150 feet, or 7,800 square feet. The various units break down as follows:

Grass	2400 sq. ft.	30%
Concrete—terraces, paths, and mowing strips	1340	18
Blacktop	2600	34
Flower border	960	12
Miscellaneous planting areas	500	6

Thus 82% of the total area is under the control of grass, concrete, and blacktop.
If it looks a little bare, remember the picture was taken six months after planting. When the planting has had several years' growth and the flower border is in bloom it will be a lush and colorful garden, with only 18% of it needing the attention of a gardener.

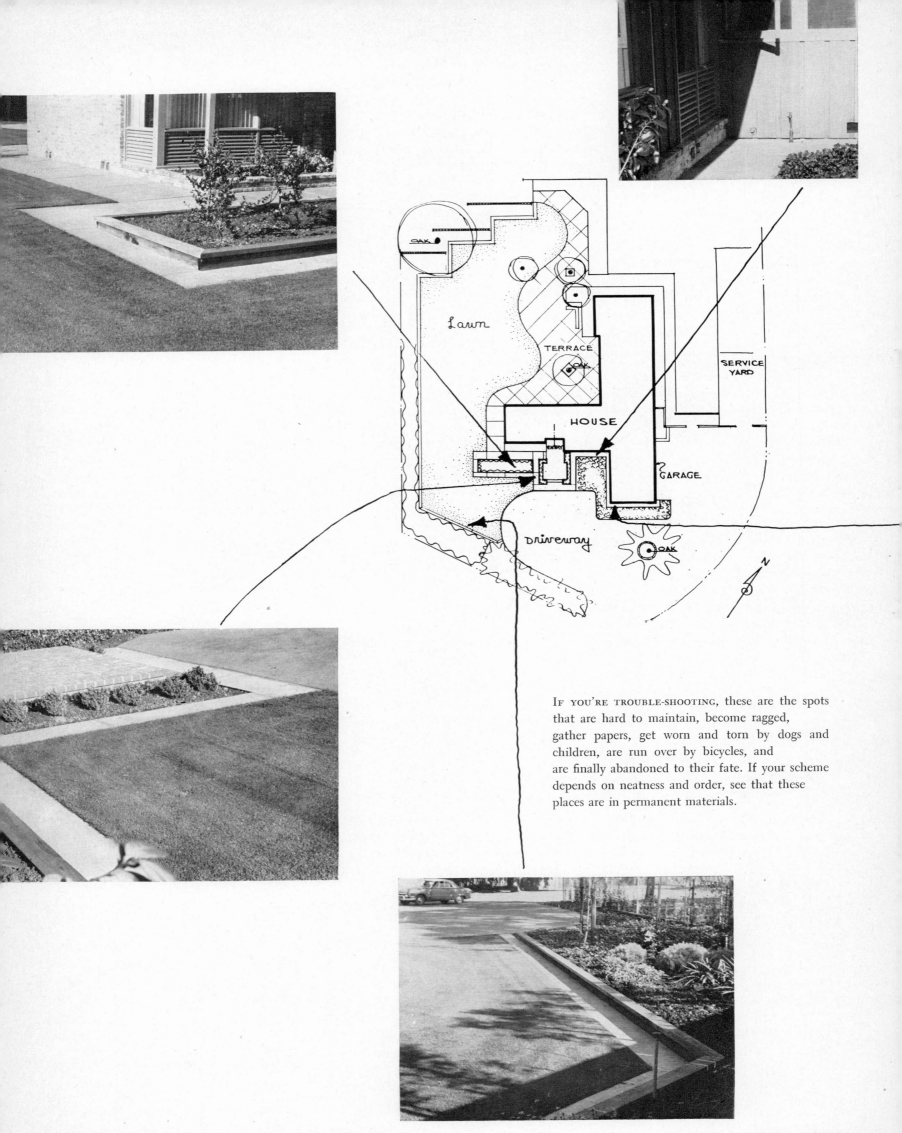

Lawn

TERRACE

OAK

OAK

SERVICE
YARD

HOUSE

ENTRY

GARAGE

Driveway

OAK

N

IF YOU'RE TROUBLE-SHOOTING, these are the spots
that are hard to maintain, become ragged,
gather papers, get worn and torn by dogs and
children, are run over by bicycles, and
are finally abandoned to their fate. If your scheme
depends on neatness and order, see that these
places are in permanent materials.

Maintenance influences both design and materials

Nothing is more pleasant to the Eye than Greene Grasse kept finely shorn. *"Of Gardens"—Francis Bacon, 1625*

. . . and with turfes new Fresh turved, whereof the grene gras So smal, so thick, so short, so fresh of hew That most like unto green wool wot I it was. *"The Flower and the Leafe"—Chaucer (1343–1400)*

People want their gardens to provide many pleasures, conveniences and comforts; none but dyed-in-the-wool gardeners want them to be any work.

There is, of course, no such thing as a 100% maintenance-free garden, and if there were, you would soon tire of it, for it would cease to be a garden. Most people mean they want the space so organized that they may know the delights of gardening in what little time they have; that they will not become a slave to a scheme that never looks its best no matter how much time they labor at it.

Large areas should be under permanent control (lawns, ground covers, paving). Most of the planting should be in permanent and slower growing materials. Frayed edges and unmanageable corners should be worked over.

Don't grasp at these straws:

"What is a good substitute for lawn?" There is none—nothing that has its bright color in contrast to other garden greens, or its texture or tactile quality. The ground covers—Lippia, Dichondra, ivy, Pachysandra, etc.—all have their place, require little care under proper conditions, and can be used to reduce the amount of lawn. Think twice, however, because once you're behind the lawn mower you might as well cut a little more, and for year-round care few materials give you so much for so little.

"Why can't I take out the grass and put in planting?" If you shift from grass to shrubs and flowers you're fooling yourself. The amount of maintenance in time and dollars will be more.

"Annuals are too much trouble, I'm going to have all perennials." But to be satisfactory, perennials also need a great deal of care. A combination of the two is probably the best answer for a maximum of color with a minimum of work.

PAVING CAN REDUCE
MAINTENANCE

*"I'm so tired of garden work I think I'll put the
whole place in concrete."*

There's no doubt that more garden space can be covered
with hard-surfaced materials and the result be
both aesthetic and practical.

The average driveway is too narrow, the parking space too
cramped, the terraces too small, and the paths too narrow; there
are places in deep shade where nothing will grow, and little-
used corners which can be paved and be the better for it. It's amazing how the amount of maintained area can be decreased.

Of course, you can't really pave your whole garden. Or can you?

As gardens are to the Japanese a vital
part of living, they must not only express the spirit and essence of nature,
but also the dignity of man. *"A
Thousand Years of Japanese Gardens"
—Samuel Newsom, 1953*

PHELPS GARDEN, ATHERTON 1952

The owner of this house paved his garden in green concrete from
one property line to the other. Was he tired of cutting his
grass? Did he lose the battle with slugs and moles? Did he, with
one final gesture, solve all his gardening problems?

In any case, he has carried the hope of reducing
maintenance to its ultimate expression.

The surest way to get into an argument is to talk about garden
maintenance, but there is one field in which it
should be increased, and that is in the care and training you give
your individual plants. Trees and shrubs are not static;
their roots and branches are continuously growing, competing for
sun and space and nitrogen with other plants, shading out
their own lower foliage, and in their enthusiasm
growing too high or in the wrong direction.

Your plants can be made objects of beauty and
grace with proper pruning and care.
Thin out weak and overcrowded plants, feed and spray, and never
walk around your garden without your pruning shears.

The eye will detect a mean dimension sooner than a generous one.— *Anon.*

Just enough flowers to take care of easily.

A simple layout is easy to care for

This garden is calm, restful, and serene, inviting contemplation. Why? Because maintenance is minimum. Hard-packed gravel was rolled for paving, and the plants are few in number but treated as friends. Any battle between a gardener and consuming foliage is not evident.

Designed for a hot dry climate, the scheme has vigor yet repose; it has a sense of belonging in nature, yet a feeling that man is at home in his surroundings.

This close relationship to natural environment is the height of true formalism; you will find it in well-tended New England woodlands, in the azalea gardens of the South, in the rocky sand gardens of Arizona, and especially in the eloquent simplicity of Japanese gardens.

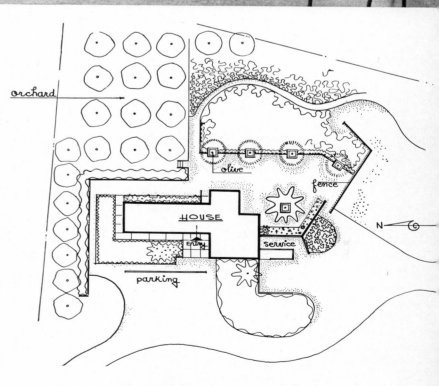

Whatsoever forme you cast it into, first it be not too Busie, or full of Worke. *"Of Gardens"* —*Francis Bacon, 1625*

CORNWALL GARDEN, SANTA BARBARA 1951

ARCHITECTS: LUTAH MARIA RIGGS & ARVIN B. SHAW III   PHOTOGRAPHER: MAYNARD PARKER

Windows affect design

No longer a slit made to fit a musket, the window
has come into its own. And modern
ingenuity has given us the picture window.
If it looks into
a secluded garden or at a view, you're
fortunate; but if it's on the front of the house, it's
the passer-by who has the view—of you.

Modern techniques give us almost unlimited
possibilities in the use of glass. They
give us the glass wall and large sliding glass panels
so a room may seem to be in the garden.
(A tendency to use large areas of glass indis-
criminately, in wrong orientations, and
under adverse conditions can turn a blessing into
a problem.)

No picture windows

The people of Monbazillac didn't
care for indoor-outdoor living. In the 14th century it meant
a spear in your back. Per-
missible were small apertures for
pouring boiling oil on un-
welcome guests, it being an age of
few inhibitions.

BLACKWOOD GARDEN, MENLO PARK, 1949; PHOTOGRAPHER: PHILIP FEIN

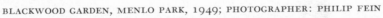

In the twentieth century
glass allows the liv-
ing room to
be part of the garden.

The deHarts had double trouble with picture windows. From the street you could see all the way through the house to the terrace. People have an insatiable curiosity about a new house, and until the screen fence was installed in the front yard, the deHarts spent their weekends in the kitchen.

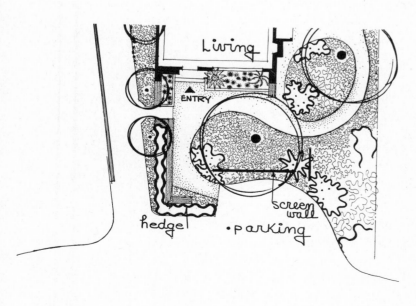

MR. & MRS. DANA C. deHART, HILLSBOROUGH 1952

LANDSCAPE CONTRACTORS: OUTDOOR CONSTRUCTION, INC.   PHOTOGRAPHER: MAYNARD PARKER   25

Views
affect design

Distant views of mountains and water, intimate views of hills and woods, views over cities at night, all have an endless fascination for people, and to get them they will search for penthouses and hilltops, install elevators, move mountains, clear forests—and build decks.

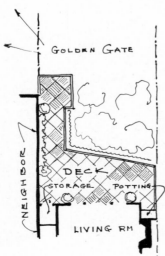

A million-dollar view of San Francisco's Golden Gate was just around the corner—of the neighbor's house.

A deck was constructed across the living room, along the house next door and forty feet above the ground, to a "crow's nest." From it, they see the Golden Gate—and, for the first time, the rear of their own house.

The living room windows, facing north, were changed to a glass wall with doors opening onto the deck.

MR. & MRS. TIREY L. FORD, SAN FRANCISCO 1949

ARCHITECT: GARDNER A. DAILEY   PHOTOGRAPHER: MAYNARD PARKER

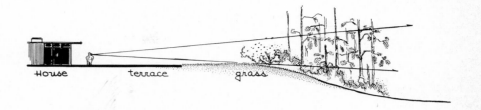

House   terrace   grass

If your lawn can roll so that it foreshortens against the view and
the surrounding landscape, you'll have
the most for your money. By
carrying the line of mowed grass over
the slope, the eye does not see
where the lawn meets the
natural ground.

THORNTON GARDEN, WESTWOOD 1949

DAVISON GARDEN, ATHERTON 1941

Put as few obstacles and diverting lines as
possible between you and your view
if you want it to retain all its drama. The
eye is fickle and easily distracted.

A curved line against a view presents the
least irritation. In this garden, a low
planting separates the lawn from the fields.
Cattle graze beyond the fence.

27

The Starks
seem to live in a
vast tree-studded lawn,
but their prop-
erty line is just 50 feet
from the house.
The country club takes
care of the grass;
they look at
it.

HOW TO ENJOY LAND YOU DON'T OWN

Man has long been concerned with keeping exuberant nature and his various
enemies out of his garden. Once his foes included wild beasts; today we
struggle with gophers, beetles, and an occasional locust.

In mediaeval times, palisades, thorn thickets, and moats were some of
the protective devices used.

Then came more benevolent times and man longed to *see* the landscape
around him and to participate in it.

MR. & MRS. WILLIAM STARK, FRESNO 1950   DESIGNER: HARRY HUNTER   PHOTOGRAPHER: MAYNARD PARKER

You may apply the theory of visual appropriation of property not your own if you live next to a park, golf-course, orchard, or meadow.

Skip that first impulse to enclose yourself with screen planting and high walls. Instead, look out at the neighboring property. Someone else is maintaining it and paying the taxes; you're enjoying it.

The Packards see this orchard in all its changing aspects; they enjoy the pattern, the flowers, and the green leaves against the brown earth. The farmer sprays, prunes, and cultivates the trees; the Packards look at them.

MR. & MRS. DAVID PACKARD, LOS ALTOS 1945

In 18th century England, cattle grazed on the public lands and were a constant and necessary part of every landscape.

To keep them out of their pleasure grounds and still see the flowing meadows and woods, a ditch with a fence at the bottom, called a "fosse" or "ha-ha," was used. This allowed the eye to move uninterruptedly over the pastoral landscape and to accept all it saw as its own.

Robert Bush doesn't want cows in his swimming pool, but like the 18th century Englishman, he likes them in his landscape. A fence was necessary, but they didn't want to see it. If they planted it out, they would lose the cows and the view.

So the fence was lowered into a ditch at the property line and the lawn rolls up to foreshorten against the meadow.

Someone else feeds and milks the cows. The Bushes look at them.

One of the melancholy appendages observable in the pleasure grounds of the past century is a long lawn without cattle. *"The Art of Landscape Gardening"—Humphrey Repton (1752–1818)*

BEFORE

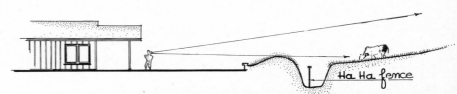

30 DR. & MRS. ROBERT N. BUSH, PALO ALTO 1954   LANDSCAPE CONTRACTORS: LOWERY & LITTLE

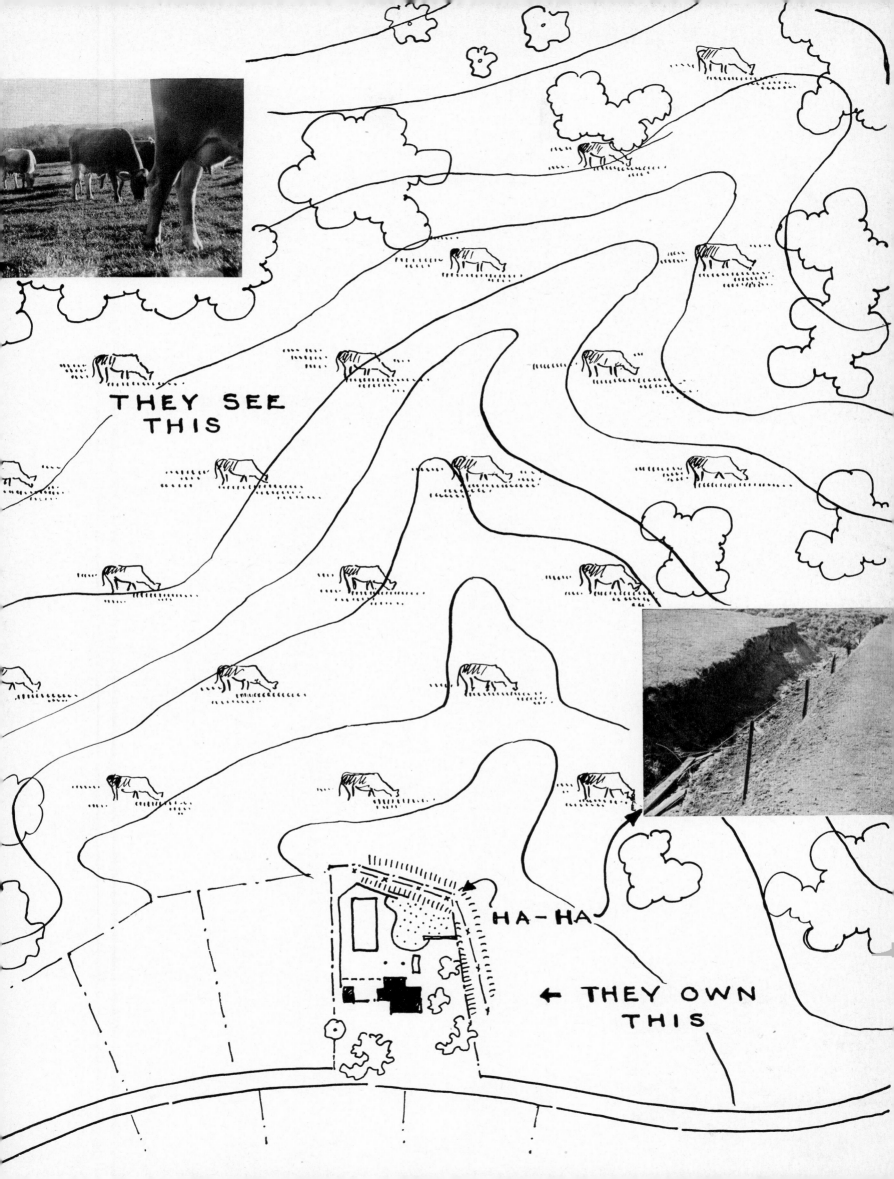

THEY SEE
THIS

HA-HA

← THEY OWN
THIS

Plants in the landscape

Trees, shrubs, vines, ground covers, and grasses cover much of the earth; knowing them and how to use them is what distinguishes the landscape architect from those in closely related fields of design.

Plants are a link with our primaeval past. They offer us shade and shadow, shelter sustenance, and give us color, texture, form, and mass to work with in our man-made compositions. Beyond this, they grow, burst into flower, drop their leaves, change color, and bear fruit.

They are a friend to man (possible exceptions, poison ivy and barrel cactus). They can be transplanted thousands of miles from their native habitat or grown for years confined in a pot for man's pleasure. They bear no resentment when severely cut; they come back again and again when constantly sheared and collaborate willingly when man's fancy turns them into pleached allees, pyramids, spirals, or peacocks.

◀ MR. & MRS. DANIEL VOLKMANN, SAN FRANCISCO 1938

PHOTOGRAPHER: RONDAL PARTRIDGE

OUR HERITAGE

CHATEAU DES CHAMPS

From centuries of man's attempt to control and beautify his surroundings, we inherit a vast knowledge of botany, horticulture, and the uses to which it has pleased him to put the flowers and plants at his disposal.

He has tried many things—from a complete and rigid control of all plant forms, with flowers providing a delicate pattern of embroidery, to a free and untrammelled expression of undisturbed nature. All have served some purpose in relating him to his times and to his surroundings.

Today we take the best from these two schools of thought (once bitter enemies)—the formal and the informal—the symmetrical and the picturesque—the geometric and the natural—the classic and the romantic.

We still have a strong tendency to control our surroundings, but in our gardens we want plants, by their structure and poetry, to suggest the fine melancholy we expect in nature. Thus do we borrow from the past.

SWEDEN

. . . for my own part, I would rather look upon a tree in all its luxuriance and diffusion of boughs and branches, than when it is thus cut and trimmed into a mathematical figure; and cannot but fancy that an orchard in flower looks infinitely more delightful, than all the little labyrinths of the most finished parterre. *"Gardens of Europe" —Osvald Sirén, 1950, quoting from "The Spectator" by Joseph Addison, 1712*

The 19th century saw the glorification of the specimen plant and the introduction of horticultural rarities throughout the world. (Douglas discovered the sequoia, and also the fir which bears his name, and sent them back to England; today you see them all over Europe.)

Americans discovered a thousand varieties and, liking the new and rare, tried them all—on the front lawn.

The Columbian Exposition in 1893 ushered in the greatest wave of "copyism" since England discovered Palladio; and our countryside was soon teeming with Italian villas, Moorish castles, and French manor houses. Architects and landscapers scurried on the Grand Tour with their rulers and notebooks. While this resulted in some fine reproductions of old-world gardens, it proved the hollowness of imitation without reason.

The Exposition des Arts Decoratif in 1925 and the Paris Fair in 1937 were brave attempts to break through the bonds of this electicism and establish a new order.

The rising tide of revolt went to excesses, as all revolutions must, and Art Moderne strangled in the mesh of its own steel tubing and alternating squares of colored pebbles and violas. The gardens of the period became the attempts of a three-dimensional art to reproduce the two-dimensional compositions of the modern painters. "Modern" was a battlecry which degenerated into a style and, finally, into a nasty word. Designers seemed to be annoyed, rather than grateful, that anyone had preceded them.

Today we are facing the last half of a century which promises a clear understanding of man's relationship to his environment. "Modern" can be revived as an honest word when we realize that Modernism is not a goal but a broad highway.

OUR IMMEDIATE INHERITANCE

      seems to be the result of the trend of the last fifty years away from the "architectural" garden to the "gardener's" garden. An intense interest in plants was naturally followed by the rise of the commercial nurseryman. The latter provided the plants and since no professional designers interested in small gardens had appeared on the scene, had to decide where and how they should be used.

The result was such dubious contributions as "the front lawn," "the open center," "the rock garden."

and—

Foundation planting

Whatever series of circumstances led to the growth and extension of this mania to camouflage our architecture, it is unfortunate that it has carried over into an era of simple houses, friendly to their surroundings and sitting on heated slabs at ground level. The foundation has disappeared, but the planting is still there.

You watch your house gradually disappear in a miasma of various foliages, which fight for light and air in front and gather leaves and cobwebs in the rear.

Or you club them into submission, using any or all of the forms remembered from your solid geometry, leaning heavily on spheres, pyramids, and cubes.

Or Start Over.

IT MAY LOOK SPARSE NOW, BUT—

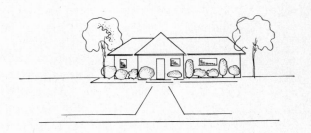

BEFORE

AFTER   HELMHOLZ GARDEN, ORINDA 1954

There *are* low evergreens and ground covers that will not get out of hand. Perhaps all you really need is a vine and an occasional plant.

Paving and grass can now approach the house without a buffer of shrubbery.

A tree, placed to frame the house or cast its shadow on it, does more "softening" than a forest of shrubs.

Heavy planting can be pushed to the boundaries, allowing the house and garden to become better acquainted.

WAIT TILL IT FILLS IN!

AFTER

THE
INEVITABLE
EXCEPTION

MENEFEE GARDEN, YAMHILL, OREGON 1946   ARCHITECT: PIETRO BELLUSCHI

A few plants and a tree to cast a shadow are all
this house requires.

HANISCH GARDEN, PASADENA 1950

ARCHITECT: HENRY L. EGGERS

PLANTING is intended to enhance architecture, not hide or
compete with it. Vines can soften its lines, plants can
create a base for it, and trees can frame it; for all are, in fact, only
part of a larger design conception.

TURNER GARDEN, MODESTO 1942

ARCHITECTS: WURSTER, BERNARDI & EMMONS

MACDOWELL GARDEN, ATHERTON 1950

ARCHITECTS: WURSTER, BERNARDI & EMMONS

Paved and kept clean at the foundation, the house preserves its dignity and the plants are out where you can really see them. It's convenient to walk around the house and easy to wash the windows.

STOCKSTROM GARDEN, ST. LOUIS, MISSOURI 1951 ARCHITECT: HARRIS ARMSTRONG PHOTOGRAPHER: EZRA STROLLER

BEFORE

AFTER   PINGREE GARDEN, LOS ANGELES

Shrubs had outgrown this space and been cut back. Perennials were tried but became messy.

Brick was the logical answer for year-round neatness, convenience, and reduced maintenance.

The existing boxwood is now a calm green line at the base of the house.

Trees are for people

In the intimate and humanized landscape, trees become the greatest single element linking us visually and emotionally with our surroundings. Other manifestations of Nature—great rocks, deserts, moors, torrents, hurricanes—stir us, fill us with awe, make us afraid or humble, but a tree we understand and can allow to become a part of us.

It's no wonder that when we first think of a garden we think of a tree.

MENUHIN—LOS GATOS

TREES AFFECT DESIGN

HANNISH—PASADENA

Trees provide a setting for many a garden vista
(into the garden, towards a view, back
to the house).

The shape of the trunk, the curve of a branch, the
texture of the foliage, the pattern of the
shade, may influence your whole design and
may determine the shape of your terrace—
where you locate the house—or whether you
even buy the property.

It is worth any amount of effort to be able to see
your house through the arch of a tree
as the Hanisches do, or to have your view
paneled by a multi-stemmed tree like the
Chinese elm at the Menuhins.

**Charles Dudley Warner said that until
he saw the Annapolis at low tide he
never realized how much it added to
the looks of a river to have water in it.
One might say the same thing of trees
in the landscape.** *"The Landscape
Beautiful"—Frank A. Waugh, 1910*

DONNELL—SONOMA
RONDAL PARTRIDGE PHOTO

TREES INFLUENCE THE PLACING OF THE HOUSE

Rockbound, windblown, and neglected, this tree seemed hardly worth saving. But we wanted it at the end of the house. It was subjected to blasting; many of its roots were cut, and scaffolding was run through the branches and around it.

But it survived, to appear two years later as you see it.

MR. & MRS. PAUL L. FAHRNEY, KENT WOODLANDS 1950

ARCHITECT: GEORGE T. ROCKRISE   PHOTOGRAPHER: MAYNARD PARKER

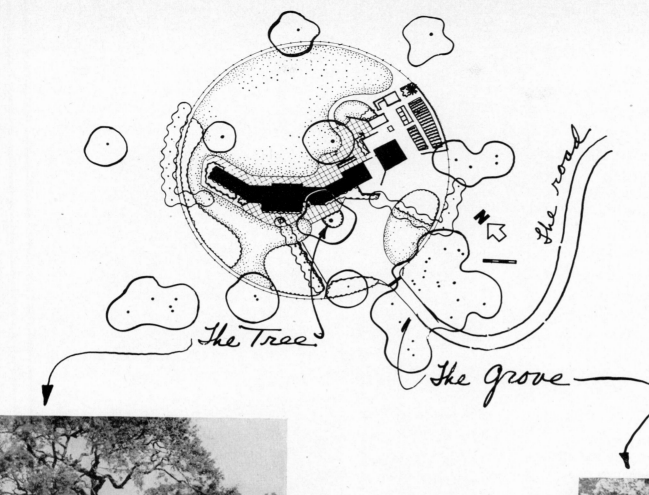

This house and garden
were built on a
large cattle ranch. An ir-
resistible tree was
enclosed by a corral fence
built in a 300-
foot circle.

The Tree

The grove

A spot near the tree was
chosen for the
main entrance to the
house.

The approach road
winds out of its way to
pass through a
grove to catch this first
glimpse of the
tree and the house to-
gether.

MR. & MRS. HARRY D. HOLT, STOCKTON 1946

ARCHITECT: JOSEPH ESHERICK   PHOTOGRAPHER: RONDAL PARTRIDGE   45

DAVIES GARDEN, WOODSIDE 1939   BIRCH

Trees
are for shadow

To list the endless fascinations of trees
would be a volume in itself, but not
the least of these is the shadows they cast.
Against buildings, onto the terrace,
and across the lawn, they provide a moving
silhouette, varying in intensity,
changing every hour.

Whether broadleaf or conifer, deciduous or
evergreen, their shadows are soft and
clustered at noon, long and dramatic at sun-
down—needed for shade, welcomed
for pattern.

LIVE OAK

PLANE

OLIVE

WHITE OAK

BALDWIN GARDEN, WOODSIDE 1939

Shadows are in reality, when the sun is shining,
the most conspicuous thing in a landscape next
to the highest lights. *"Painting"—John Ruskin*
(1819–1900)

Look carefully at your trees to be sure you have developed all they
have to give you. Their beauty is not in foliage alone but
in their shape and branching and in the relation of their structure
to their foliage. It's pleasant and very exciting to look *up*
into a tree and *through* a tree, as well as *at* it.

'Trimming up' instead of cutting out is the common error of persons ignorant of the arts of sylvan picture-making. *"Suburban Home Grounds"—F. J. Scott, 1870*

TREES CAN BE

LIVING SCULPTURE

All the trees here were once in trouble. They took up too much space in the garden, or their bulk was oppressive, or they hid distant views or flower borders. Many times a tree *should* come out, but often the bulk and weight are only in the foliage, and investigation will disclose unrevealed beauty in the branches.

Since the volume of air space in a garden is just as important as the volume of foliage, you may gain more than you realize in scale by lifting the foliage line, clearing out the center or even reshaping the tree by major surgery.

If you belong to the school which believes that every leaf on a tree is sacred and every branch removed is a violation of nature, you're nice, but you're neither a competent arborist nor a good artist. Pruning to accent the strong natural forms of the trunks and branches does your tree no harm. The dead and dying wood, the small and weak shoots, the "double-duty" branches are actually a burden to it.

Study the tree earnestly. Don't just hack away at the branches that scratch your car or catch in your hairnet. If in doubt, don't be hasty. It's easier to take off a limb than to put it back on again.

And remember, you're not just pruning a tree. You are creating an artistic triumph that's just as important to you and your garden's success as sculpture was to Vaux-le-Vicompte.

Pruning shears, wisely used, are the gardener's best friend.

The palette

Rich in tradition and colorful in content, the
landscape architect's palette is more
varied and provocative than that offered to
any other designer. He has the benefit
of the best of man's efforts in architecture,
horticulture, and the fine arts; and
he has the materials and resources of the
natural world at his disposal.

The design

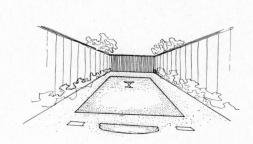

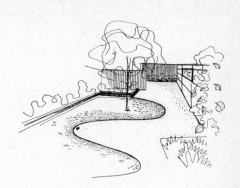

To fill that space with objects of beauty, to delight the eye after it has been struck, to fix the attention where it has been caught, to prolong astonishment into admiration, are purposes not unworthy of the greatest designs. *"The Art of Landscape Gardening" Humphrey Repton, 1795*

Your solution will depend upon the site conditions, the house, and your own personality and preferences.

Whether your design is "formal" or "informal," curved or straight, symmetrical or free, or a combination of all, the important thing is that you end up with a functional plan and an artistic composition. It must have good proportion and proper scale and plants that have been chosen wisely and cared for affectionately.

Rhythm and movement are essential. You expect them in the pictures you hang on your wall, in the music you listen to, in the poetry you read. In the garden it's the wind in the foliage and the dog running across the lawn. It's the line of the terrace and the repetition of richly-textured foliage. The eye is a restless organ.

Symmetry can have motion. It's unimaginative "formality" that can become static. The eye prefers to move around a garden on lines that are provocative, never lose their interest, never end in dead corners, occasionally provide excitement or surprise, and always leave you interested—and contented.

Someone may say "I don't want it formal, laid out on an axis."

The truth is your garden is never without at least one axis and probably has two or three. All compositions, however free, are built around them. The great designers of natural gardens may seem to have thrown away their T squares, but the axis is just as strong as in the mirror pool of the Taj Mahal. It's just less obvious.

The axis becomes visual rather than mechanical and needn't be at right angles to the eye. The eye is tolerant. It may be influenced by a view, nudged by a tree, encouraged by a meadow, or seduced by a brook. Don't fret if your garden is never quite perfect. Absolute perfection, like complete consistency, can be dull.

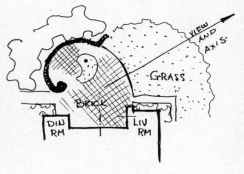

The Jerd Sullivan garden in San Francisco, shown in the photograph, left, and plan above, is to be seen from a second-story living room rather than to be used constantly. It makes use of strong, year-round pattern in paving, walls, and planting, with a minimum of seasonal color.

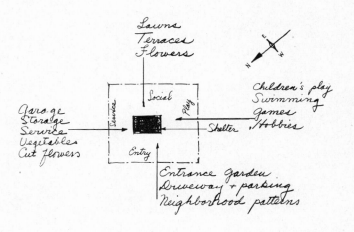

The eye, or rather the mind, is never long delighted with that which it surveys without effort, at a single glance, and therefore sees without exciting curiosity or interest. *"The Art of Landscape Gardening" —Humphrey Repton, 1795*

MR. & MRS. EARL S. DOUGLASS, JR., SAN FRANCISCO 1941

CHAPTER TWO

The tour

The gardens you will see in this chapter range from small town gardens to fairly large (for today) country places. The tour will include modest gardens for tract houses, remodeled gardens for old houses, and more elaborate schemes where space and funds were not limited.

You will be shown the owners' problems, their desires, and the final solutions.

When the tour is over, may you feel that having a garden is a pleasure and that gardening, in whatever degree you indulge, is rewarding.

The Douglasses have a quiet, colorful garden in the center of the city. From their dining room they look across flagstone to a hillside terraced in river-washed sandstone and planted in spring bulbs. A flowering crab apple arches over the steps.
Ivy grows at the base of the house next door to make a green background.

A city garden, especially of one who has no other, ought to be planted and ornamented with all possible care.—*Cato (234–149* B.C.)

FLOWER CONSULTANT: LAURA MERCADO SMITH

STONE MASON: ANGELO ANTONIAZZI   PHOTOGRAPHER: MAYNARD PARKER

THE GEORGE EVANSES OWNED

A TYPICAL BACK YARD

It was the All-American back yard of a few years ago, mostly lawn
surrounded by flowers, with several fruit trees.

There was a large shade tree near the house. A path of stepping
stones wandered across the lawn, around a flower bed, and
to a rockery and pool in one corner. Behind the garage was a
convenient catch-all with a miscellany of lumber, odd
lengths of pipe, and an abandoned doghouse.

The garden was like hundreds of unpretentious small
yards from coast to coast which had triumphed
over the earlier American idea that the back yard was
a place to dump the ashes.

It was "landscaped," and they liked their lily pool.
But the Evanses were not happy.

It took too much time and care to keep it looking well the year
round. There was no terrace for comfortable furniture,
and they needed more space for entertaining. The shade tree was
in the wrong place, making the bedroom dark and casting no shade on the garden. The garbage cans and back
door were too much in evidence. They wanted to get
from the living room to the garden without crowding between
the house and the hedge. The entrance side,
sunny in winter, had no privacy.

Their restlessness resulted in a solution which corrected most of
their complaints. Now there's a large terrace, a new door
from the living room, a path to the garden, and
a better setting for the lily pool.
But best of all, there is more time to relax.

One not so fortunate as to possess a
commanding site could nevertheless
make a pretty landskip of his own
possessions. *"The Spectator"—Joseph
Addison (1672–1719)*

MR. & MRS. GEORGE L. EVANS, PALO ALTO 1946

PHOTOGRAPHER: RONDAL PARTRIDGE

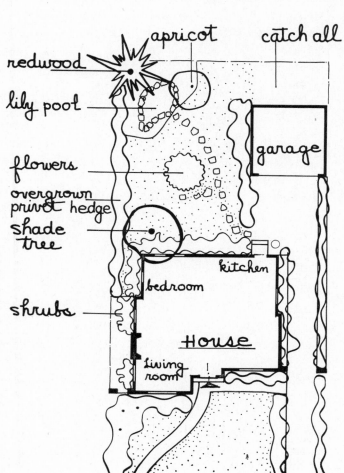

redwood
apricot
catch all
lily pool
garage
flowers
overgrown privet hedge
shade tree
kitchen
bedroom
shrubs
House
living room

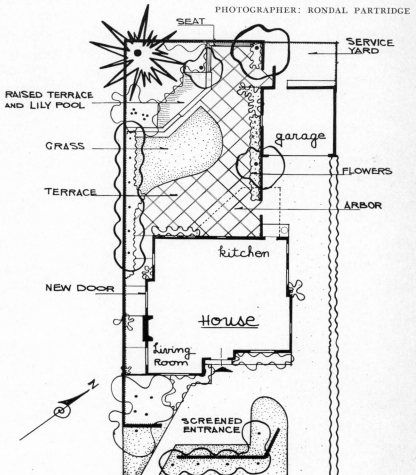

SEAT
SERVICE YARD
RAISED TERRACE AND LILY POOL
garage
GRASS
FLOWERS
TERRACE
ARBOR
kitchen
NEW DOOR
House
Living Room
SCREENED ENTRANCE

57

Taylor Bradford bought a tract house and drew a sketch of what
he wanted. "If it's O.K., I'll build it," he said.
"If not, tell me why, and I'll listen."

They wanted what all young couples buying tract
houses want—barbecue, terrace, play space for children,
shed for tools, and some lawn and flowers.

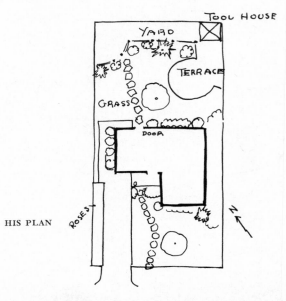

HIS PLAN

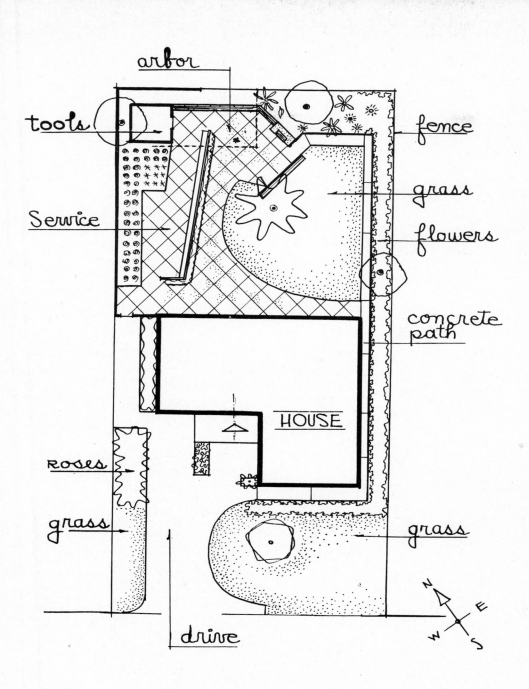

arbor

tools

Service

Roses

grass

fence

grass

flowers

concrete path

HOUSE

grass

drive

N E S W

As the plan developed, the service areas and play space moved closer to the kitchen door, as did the barbecue, to make serving easier.

The terrace moved too, so as not to face the sun, and the tool house roof was extended over it for more shade. The flower border is along the sunny side of the fence.

There is ample concrete paving for entertaining and for children. A concrete band runs along the lawn and all around the house to the driveway. It keeps the children out of the mud and keeps the base of the house dry and clean.

The house Floyd Gerow bought was like thousands of other $10,000 GI houses. It was ordinary but sound; the lot was good but uncultivated and unfenced. A picture window faced a paralyzing western exposure.

MR. & MRS. FLOYD GEROW, PALO ALTO 1952

The owner of a small cottage residence may have almost every kind of beauty in his grounds that the largest estate will afford, so far as regards the interest of trees and plants, tasteful arrangement, recreation and occupation. *"A Treatise on the Theory and Practice of Landscape Gardening" —A. J. Downing with supplement by Henry Winthrop Sargent, 1859*

No novice at landscaping (Gerow is a landscape contractor), his garden is not only well-executed but perfectly maintained as well. Flower beds are raised, and garden surfaces are in pebble concrete and grass. The service yard and vegetable garden are paved in asphalt.

His only complaints are that he's too busy to sit on his terrace as much as he'd like and that his wife, an expert on flower arrangements, keeps his vegetable beds filled with flowers.

He admits that keeping the garden in bloom all year takes some work, but so far he enjoys it. If he ever becomes a really lazy gardener, he'll change to permanent planting.

MORE ▶

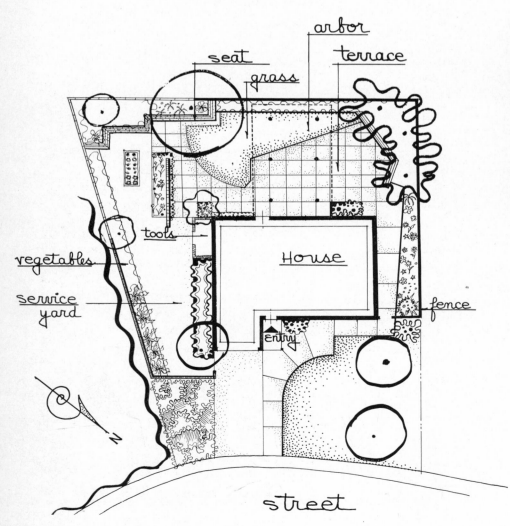

Before this sunshade was built, the Gerows had to draw the blinds on the big window until the sun went down.

The arbor extends from the house to the lot line (32 feet). The first section from the house is solid, to shade the window, and the rest is open lath.

Fences are stained black to create an illusion of more space.

MR. & MRS. FLOYD GEROW

A TOWN GARDEN

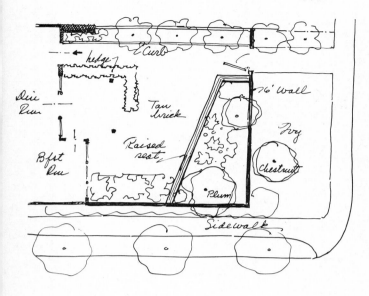

Often, especially in town, the front of the house may be the only open space or have the only acceptable exposure. Here, the architects put the house on the back of the lot, saving the street side for a south garden, protected from the wind.

A seven-foot concrete wall (showing the pattern of the form lumber) screens the court from the street. A row of trees arches over the entrance walk.

The garden space (about 30′ x 36′) had to include an entrance from the street to the front door, a terrace for dining and sunning with some privacy, a few trees and flowers, and a screen against the house next door.

A hedge of waxleaf privet (Ligustrum texanum) separates the entry from the terrace. The select tan pavers are laid tight-joint on a sand base. The seat and curbs are stained dark brown (Cabot's Creosote Stain #250).

Light walls come forward; dark walls tend to recede.

Here, the existing stucco and tile wall was covered with resawn redwood and stained dark to make it seem farther away.

Two Victorian box (Pittosporum undulatum) will complete screening of the house next door.

COQ HARDI

TOURS

Nor is the imagination so fastidious as to take offense at any well-supported deception, even after the want of reality is discovered. *"The Art of Landscape Gardening"*—Humphrey Repton, 1795

MRS. ALEXANDER ALBERT, SAN FRANCISCO 1952

SCULPTOR: ADALINE KENT

BEFORE

◄ AFTER

CITY GARDENS have many complications not found in country places—cramped areas, dense shadows, towering neighbors, and cold drafts.

Agnes Albert had most of these, as well as French doors opening from her dining room into a garden area nine and one-half feet wide, surrounded by a wall four feet high. The neighbor's back door was the center of interest.

Forced perspective, as a trick in trelliage design, was used on the flat surface to gain an illusion of distance.

BEFORE

AFTER

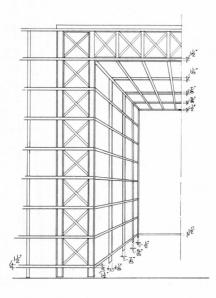

Towards his study and bedchamber joynes a little garden, which tho' very narrow, by the addition of a well painted perspective is to appearance greatly enlarged. It is a very agreeable deceipt.—*John Evelyn, describing the garden of the Count de Liancourt, 1642*

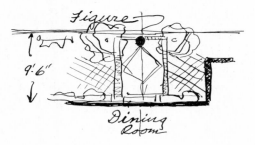

LANDSCAPE CONTRACTOR: ALEC CATTINI

AFTER PHOTOS: MAYNARD PARKER

A NEW STRUCTURE IN AN OLD GARDEN

"Do we *have* to copy the style of the old house when we build our pool house?" That's what Phyllis and Graeme MacDonald wanted to know when they planned to expand into the garden.

You can if you want to, but you certainly don't have to. Garden houses, guest houses, bathhouses, doghouses, and mail boxes, done as miniatures of the big house, can become too quaint.
Any resemblance to the entrance to toyland is suspect.

Neither do you have to insult your present house by implication and fly off in a totally new and daring direction.

When the MacDonalds built a garden house they chose simple materials, stained wood and stone, which blend with the old house. It's modern, but that isn't its first statement.

Mountains of ancient shrubbery were removed to get a flowing lawn and a site for the new garden house and pool. The large live oak, buried for years in evergreens and vines, now dominates the scene and is a friendly companion for the low, flat-roofed pavilion.

You think about adding a swimming pool when
you have five growing boys.

It led the MacDonalds to think further and plan an entertainment
center, with fireplace, barbecue, summer kitchen,
and dressing rooms which can double as small dormitories.

The grey-blue tree is Eucalyptus pulverulenta.

MR. & MRS. GRAEME MacDONALD, SAN MATEO 1949

A COUNTRY GARDEN for people who want to do a reasonable amount of controlled gardening and a generous amount of relaxing.

There's space for a border of color, a vegetable garden, and a pot rack to display geraniums.

Behind the board and batten fence (which screens an undesirable view) is a garden work area with tools, potting bench, greenhouse, and storage.

The vegetable beds are level and step down the slope. One is used as a sandbox while the children are small. Two have benches at one end for work space.

MORE ▶

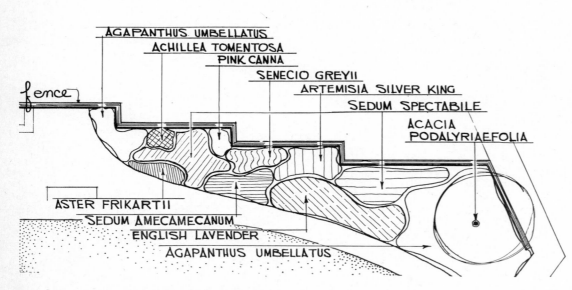

AGAPANTHUS UMBELLATUS
ACHILLEA TOMENTOSA
PINK CANNA
SENECIO GREYII
ARTEMISIA SILVER KING
SEDUM SPECTABILE
ACACIA PODALYRIAEFOLIA

fence

ASTER FRIKARTII
SEDUM AMECAMECANUM
ENGLISH LAVENDER
AGAPANTHUS UMBELLATUS

The color border at the de-Brettevilles' is planted in hardy, long-blooming perennials with blue, yellow, and white predominating. Foliage varies from the bright green of the agapanthus to the pale yellow-green of the sedums; from the grey of the lavender and acacia to the near-white of the artemesia. There is always color, in either flower or foliage, from spring to late fall.

Over the pot rack and the tanbark terrace is a sunshade of steel and lath, from which hang
baskets of fuchsias, begonias, and campanulas.

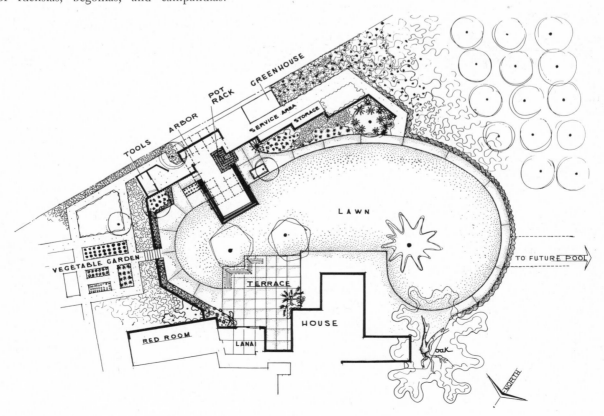

PHOTOGRAPHER: RONDAL PARTRIDGE

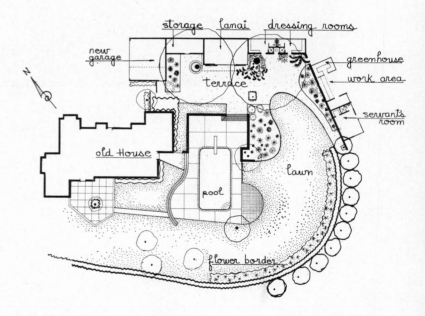

ADDITIONS TO AN OLD HOUSE WERE BUILT AROUND THE GARDEN

The Jasons bought an old house on a fine site with large trees, but the house was too small.

They needed a servant's room, a larger garage, more storage, a small greenhouse, and a swimming pool and dressing rooms.

These additions, using the dramatic old white oaks to frame the lanai, were built around the pool and garden.

The flower border is Mrs. Jason's great pride. Planted mostly in annuals, it is changed three times a year. In late summer there are petunias, zinnias, tall and dwarf marigolds, with the second bloom of the delphiniums.

BEFORE

THE LANAI

PHOTOGRAPHER: PHILIP FEIN

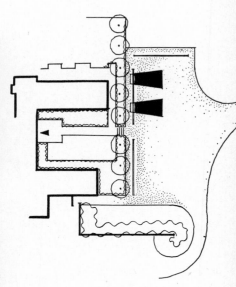

MR. & MRS. RICHARD H. SHAINWALD, ATHERTON 1949
ARCHITECTS: WURSTER, BERNARDI & EMMONS
PHOTOGRAPHER: FRED LYON

MR. & MRS. RICHARD A. HOEFER, BRONXVILLE, N. Y. 1952
ARCHITECT: HENRY L. EGGERS
PHOTOGRAPHER: MAYNARD PARKER

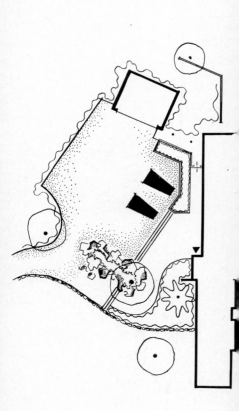

CHAPTER THREE

The arrival—welcome!

The psychology of arrival is more important than you think.

If it is not obvious where to park, if there is no room to park when you get there, if you stumble into the back door looking for the front entrance, or if the entrance is badly lighted, you have subjected your guests to a series of annoyances which will linger long in their subconscious.

No matter how warm your hearth or how beautiful your view, the over-all effect will be dimmed by these first irritations.

There is commonly a great propensity to make the sweeps of gravel at an entrance door for carriages to turn in a good deal too large for the accommodation of careless coachmen. . . . The smaller the space that can possibly be turned in the better it will look.
"Landscape Gardening"—Kemp, 1850

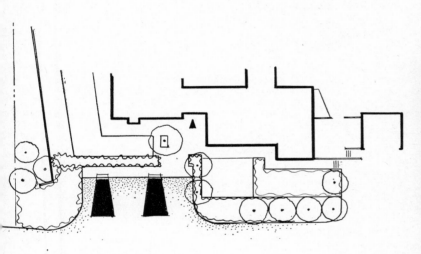

MR. & MRS. RICHARD B. RICHMOND, SAN JOSE 1951
ARCHITECTS: WURSTER, BERNARDI & EMMONS
PHOTOGRAPHER: FRED LYON

MR. & MRS. HAROLD E. KOERBER, HILLSBOROUGH 1950
PHOTOGRAPHER: FRED LYON

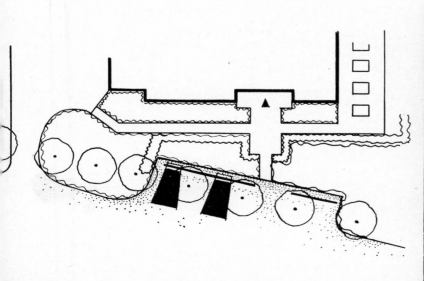

The Turners wanted privacy from the street and yet to have their guests arrive pleasantly and park easily.

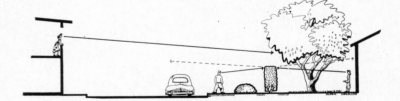

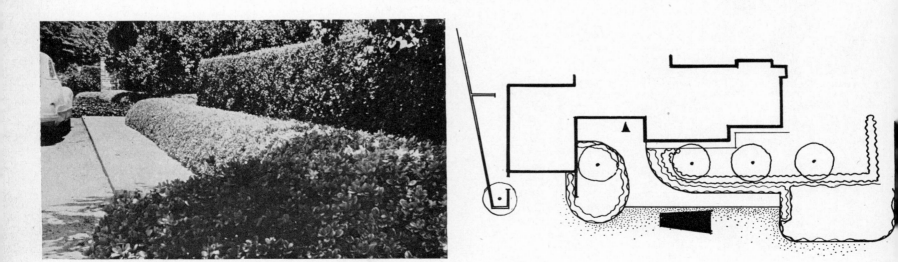

MR. & MRS. EVERETT TURNER, MODESTO 1942

ARCHITECTS: WURSTER, BERNARDI & EMMONS   PHOTOGRAPHER: PHILIP FEIN

SWEDEN

DON'T HIDE THE FRONT DOOR

Suggest, by its size, color, and design, which door is the main entrance.

The lines of the paths and planting, too, may be used to increase its importance.

SWEDEN

MR. & MRS. WELLINGTON HENDERSON, HILLSBOROUGH 1934
ARCHITECTS: WURSTER, BERNARDI & EMMONS   PHOTOGRAPHER: ROGER STURTEVANT   77

HAWKINS GARDEN, ATHERTON   ALL ASPHALT

"The front walk" is not necessarily a defined and regular pathway. It may splay outward to provide additional room and suggest more welcome.

Too often the drive, the walk, and the entry platform are of three different materials. Simplify the scheme by using only one.

Serpentine or wavy lines may be regarded as the characteristic feature of the new style. Its object is beauty of line and general variety . . . It has all the grace of nature without its ruggedness and the refinement of art apart from its stiffness and severity. *"Landscape Gardening" — Kemp, 1850*

Curving paths cannot be right, for the Chinese themselves, with whom the landscape style began, make their paths straight, arguing that they must be due either to design or to repeated passage, that no sober man will deliberately propose to reach his destination by a series of curves. *"On the Making of Gardens" —Sir George Sitwell, 1909*

ENTRANCE WALKS

If you are an admirer of the American Indian (whose squaw followed several paces to the rear) you'll prefer to have your walk the size of a trail. Or are you assuming all your guests are madly in love?

Even this fine careless attitude does not justify making an obstacle race out of the trip from the car to the front door.

It will require the finest food and the most comfortable chair to make up for being pushed into the mud or having your hat knocked off by overhanging trees and your nylons ripped on the pyracantha.

The size of walks, arrival areas, and platforms must be adjusted to the scale of the building. But in all cases, there should be enough room for a group of people to wait for the bell to be answered or to linger over good-byes.

The guest should always feel that the act of arriving has been effortless.

BEFORE

THE TRACT HOUSE

Little or no attention seems to have been given to the site improvements of the small lot in large subdivisions.

A Letter to a Builder

Dear Sir:

I am pleased to find a builder who will include in his basic price certain features which I feel have been neglected and which will probably never get done by the ultimate owner.

These are:

1. An integrated driveway and front entrance scheme, so that too many different materials will not appear in a small front yard. You will

AFTER

BRADFORD GARDEN, SAN JO

EICHLER HOMES, GREENMEADOW TRACT, PALO ALTO 1954

notice that the front porch, the front walk, and the driveway are obviously never studied in relation to each other.

2. Paving completely around the house, with some obvious exceptions. This allows non-muddy access to the house, eliminates splash onto the siding, provides drainage away from the footings, lets windows be washed without trampling the shrubbery, and puts most of the planting three or four feet away from the house.

3. A paved service yard, screened from the street but easily reached from the kitchen and laundry.

4. A terrace area, properly oriented and well related to the house layout.

The balance of the lot can be easily landscaped by the owner into grass, flower beds, trees, shrubbery, vegetables, play areas, etc., without spoiling the basic relation of the house to the site.

Very truly yours,

EFORE   GEROW GARDEN, PALO ALTO   AFTER

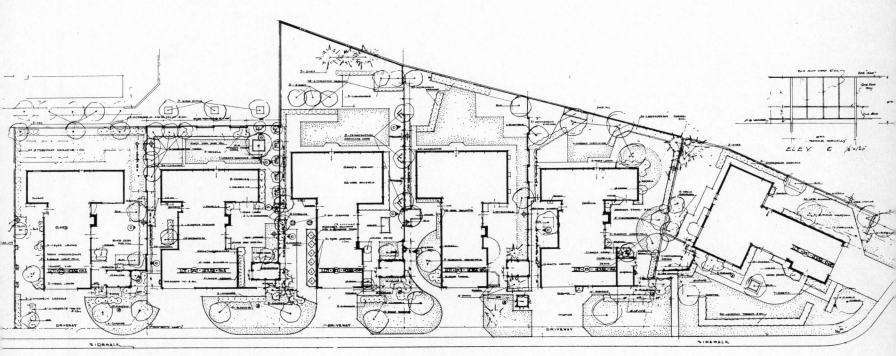

PLAN SHOWING DRIVEWAYS INTEGRATED WITH ENTRANCES—GREENMEADOW TRACT

AN ENTRANCE GARDEN

An enclosed court-garden makes a delightful entrance, and it's even more delightful if a garden gate and a covered walk insure privacy and protection.

This garden, also a morning terrace, consists of existing boulders, a few plants, and asphalt paving.

MISS ALICE ERVING, SANTA BARBARA 1951

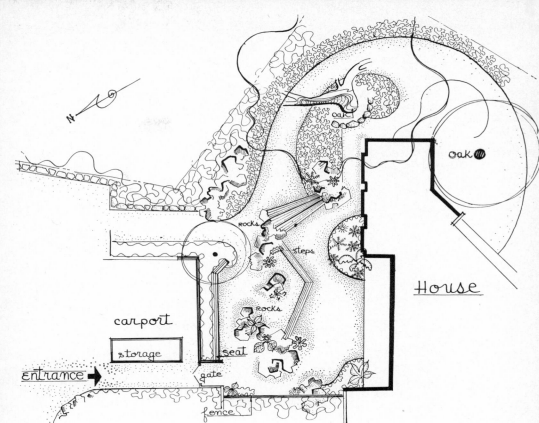

carport

storage

House

rocks

steps

seat

entrance

gate

fence

ARCHITECTS: LUTAH MARIA RIGGS & ARVIN B. SHAW, III

PHOTOGRAPHER: MAYNARD PARKER

The terrace

in all periods of gardening, and whether called atrium, close, promenade, or lanai, has been an obviously man-made part of the garden. It has been used to extend the architectural lines of the house and supplement the activities of the occupants. Today "terrace" is used as an all-inclusive term to denote an area for outdoor living.

In Pompeii, the terrace was an inside court, surrounded by the rooms of the house. It was simple and severe, cooled by the sound of water, and removed from the noises of the street.

The enclosed court was used throughout the Middle Ages when it was unwise to venture outside the walls. In Spain, as the patio, it reached its highest development as a decorative adjunct to the house. Here they had sun or shade, fresh air, cooling fountains, fruit trees, colorful vines and potted plants, and above all, seclusion and privacy.

In the large formal gardens developed after the 16th century, the terrace was an intermediate stop between the house and a vast complex of formal parterres. The gardens were large—grandeur and great scale were the order of the day. They could hold large crowds; Louis XIV gave a party on the terraces of Versailles for three thousand people which lasted for three days.

Our terraces today are also for entertaining and must be in scale with what we expect them to do for us.

VERSAILLES

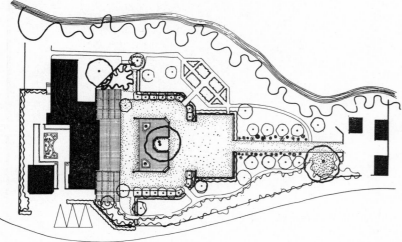

This scheme borrows line and simplicity of layout from the French formal gardens but is reduced in size to fit modern living.

Planned as a green garden, it is surrounded by a yew hedge and hawthornes. Small boxwood parterres with bright color are in the center of the sunken garden.

The terrace is sunk below the lawn to get under the branches of the oak tree. It is shaded when the house terrace is in full sun and provides interest on an otherwise flat lot.

The brick retaining wall doubles as a seat.

MR. & MRS. WELLINGTON HENDERSON, HILLSBOROUGH 1934   PHOTOGRAPHER: MAYNARD PARKER   85

To adequately plan a gentleman's country place, with the terraces and parterres in fashion today, will require a minimum of thirty acres. *"The Theory and Practice of Gardening"—Alexander LeBlond, from the Paris edition by John James, London, 1728*

MR. & MRS. BOB HOPE, NORTH HOLLYWOOD 1950   **LANDSCAPE CONTRACTOR: FLOYD MATTHEWS**

THE TERRACE MAY BE FLOWING OR FORMAL IN OUTLINE

It is no longer thought of as a small rectangle directly off the living room; it may go around the house or wander over a large portion of the lot.

It may reach out some distance and at seemingly odd and unpredictable angles, seeking a tree for shade, securing a vantage point for a view, or avoiding rough topography.

It can be generous in extent or intimate in feeling; not so big that it looks like a "corporation yard" nor so small that one is pushed into the flower beds.

It can encompass grass plots, flower beds, potted plants, arbors, sun platforms, wind screens, sand for the children, and a drinking fountain for the dog.

It should have comfortable furniture with convenient storage and easy access to the living room and kitchen.

The terrace should do all these things, as well as put some people in the sun, some in the shade, and others out of a draft.

MR. & MRS. LEONARD M. SPERRY, LOS ANGELES 1953   PLANTING: EVANS & REEVES   87

Terraces are for entertaining

Today, with the average extent of our properties
lying between the fifty-foot lot and
the suburban acre, any likeness between us
and Louis XIV has disappeared, except that we
too like to give garden parties.

And parties and terraces were made for each other.

They might have to look well with a few
people for bridge or a dozen for a barbecue; they
may need room for forty people after the
Big Game, or once a year a hundred for cocktails.

Adequate seating and good food contribute to the
success of any party on any terrace.

And of course the success of any terrace depends
on how comfortable you feel on it—when
there is no party.

As to the Size of the garden
. . . seven or eight acres is as
much as any gentlemen need
design, and will furnish as
much of all that is expected
from it as any nobleman will
have occasion to use in his
family. *"Upon the Gardens of
Epicurus"—Sir William Temple (1628–1700); quoted from
"The Garden as Considered in
Literature by certain polite
writers" with a critical essay
by Walter Howe, 1890*

. . . four to five acres
will afford ground
enough to give all the
finer pleasures of rural
life. *"Suburban Home
Grounds"—F. J. Scott,
1870*

And now to sum up as
to a garden. Large or
small, it should look
both orderly and rich
. . . . It follows from
this, that no private
pleasure garden should
be very big. . . .
*"Hopes and Fears for
Art"—William Morris
(1834–1896)*

The terrace extends into the Hoefers' garden room. It can be open to the garden or converted to a screened porch by movable panels.

Night lighting increases the use of the garden for summer parties. Their terrace is lighted by three swivel lights set on tall aluminum poles painted black.

SUPPER IN THE GARDEN

BREAKFAST IN THE SUN

A DOZEN FOR BUFFET

A FEW FOR COCKTAILS

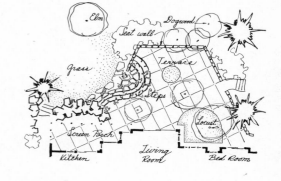

MR. & MRS. RICHARD A. HOEFER, BRONXVILLE, N. Y. 1952

ARCHITECT: HENRY L. EGGERS   PHOTOGRAPHER: MAYNARD PARKER

A small brick terrace has come down under the trees to be nearer the view, to be in shade, to get a pleasant vista back to the house, and to start you out on the five-minute promenade which encircles the house.

A TERRACE MAY BE

AWAY FROM THE HOUSE

When possible, a part of the terrace should be far enough away
so that the view back to the house is pleasant. The areas
around it compose best only from a certain distance. If your terrace is small and you sit with your back to your own house,
you may look only at your neighbor's.

If your neighbor's house is better looking than
yours, don't read any farther.

Try walking around your house. In some places, you will walk
fast, but sooner or later you will reach a spot where you
feel in repose. It may be the lines of the house or
the position of trees, or you may never know why; but it
could be the place for your terrace.

WATERS GARDEN, HILLSBOROUGH 1950

Here a circular piece of the house terrace has been carved out and
transplanted under the oaks and redwoods. It gets morning
shade and afternoon sun (the reverse of the main terrace).

MR. & MRS. DANA C. de HART, HILLSBOROUGH 1952

This terrace stays on level ground in concrete squares as long as it can, then breaks into a wood deck to go under the tree and terminates in a seat from which there's an excellent view of the house.

Bedroom, living room, and kitchen open onto the double terrace, one in sun and one in shade.

The seat at the end of the wood deck is open, to show as much planting as possible.

It ought to lie to the best Parts of the House, or to those of the Master's Commonest Use, so as to be but like one of those Rooms out of which you step into another. *"Of Gardening"—Sir William Temple (1628–1700)*

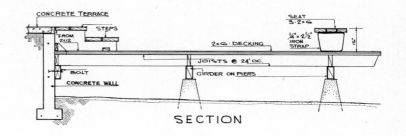

Section showing construction of concrete and wood terrace.

The problems of design, orientation, and materials vary enormously in different parts of the country.

In some sections, the garden and terrace may be 90 per cent paved and be a logical solution. In others, the lawn may be the terrace.

The problem may be protection from wind in San Francisco, or reaching out for a breeze in St. Louis. It may be designed largely for use at night in Texas, or require screening in the mosquito belt. It may need shade most of the time, or sun most of the time (the terrace large enough for both is ideal).

If you are discreet, you will realize that one terrace, well kept up, is much more valuable than several left in disrepair. *"The Garden"—Albert Maumone, Gardens of Today—Paris, 1932*

A covered walk between the house and garage has been enlarged to make a comfortable terrace. It's near the kitchen for serving and has a bar at one end. There's a swimming pool in the lawn to the left.

MR. & MRS. DAVID D. BOHANNON, WOODSIDE 1938   ARCHITECT: GARDNER A. DAILEY

This terrace garden, although largely paved, has a
lush quality supplied by a minimum of
planting and a scattering of potted
plants.

Since the house was built into an existing orchard,
the terrace is surrounded by fruit trees.

**Some fine Pavement about it,
doeth well.** *"Of Gardens"—
Francis Bacon (1561–1626)*

MR. & MRS. EVERETT TURNER, MODESTO 1942

BEFORE

The Grunskys had a small lot in town, but they didn't enjoy it. It had definite assets—an arbor covered with wisteria, a shade tree, a door leading from the living room to the garden.

But they couldn't see into the garden from the house; there was very little privacy from the street or the neighbors and nothing grew well.

AFTER

These few changes gave them what they wanted:

1. The door was changed to a single panel and the corner of the living room was changed to glass.
2. A solid board fence was built across the front and side property lines.
3. The terrace was extended around the side to give the living room the effect of sitting in the garden.
4. A brick seat was built around the tree.
5. The planting bed along the wall was filled with azaleas. Vines will be trained on the fences.

Love your neighbor, but pull not down your fences.—*George Herbert* (1563–1632)

Outdoor living in an enclosed courtyard, an old Spanish custom, provides the ultimate in privacy, protection, and accessibility.

The court above is a center for family living. The main rooms of the house lead into it, and it is easily served from the kitchen.

Wide sliding doors can be opened for a breeze or closed when it's windy. When it's cool, there is radiant heat in the floor and an open campfire in the center of the court.

However small it is on the surface, it is four thousand miles deep; and that is a very handsome property.
My Summer in a Garden—Charles Dudley Warner, 1870

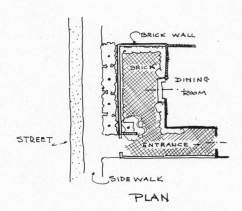

PLAN

The Metcalfs had the typical ten or twelve feet between their house and the city sidewalk.

A catch-all for papers and dogs, it was exposed to the street and flooded with morning sunshine.

Now the wall gives privacy, and clipped trees create a screen from the windows across the street. Dining room windows were changed to doors. Breakfast there is a pleasure.

There do I either Study, or Walk, or Talk with a Friend, or Eat a Dish of Meat, according as the Humour takes me.—*Erasmus (1467–1536)*

PUT A SMALL TERRACE

WHERE YOU'LL USE IT

There may be special-purpose terraces other than the main living terrace.

Small, quiet places to read the morning paper, eat, knit, sunbathe, or shell the peas may be outside any door or deep in the garden. Their location is a matter of convenience.

If the terrace is for eating—it should be easily reached from the kitchen (unless it's for picnics and hiking to it is considered an excursion).

If it's for sleeping—it should be quiet with trees strategically placed for swinging a hammock.

If it's for sun-bathing—it should be private and sheltered from the wind.

If it's for drinking—it should be level.

You must look for conditions that suit the special purpose of the terrace—a point from which there is a view hidden from the house, or where the sun shines at a certain hour; a spot where there's an afternoon breeze in the summer, or where there is protection from the wind in the fall; or an area that makes a sun pocket in the snow.

Move in and live with your property before you make all the decisions.

WALLACE GARDEN, SAN FRANCISCO, 1941

SULLIVAN GARDEN, SARATOGA, 1940

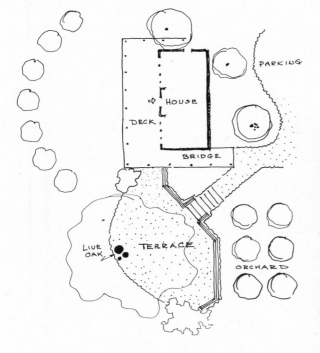

A week-end house with a sunny
deck needed this lower
shaded terrace under a live oak
tree.

99

A LINE CAN LEAD YOUR EYE AROUND A CORNER

By a curve or an angle or any strong combination of lines in plants and structural materials, the designer may lead the eye in any direction he chooses.

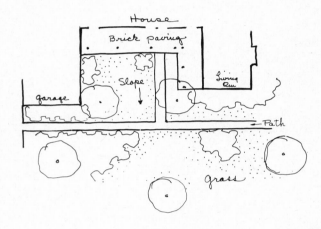

The existing court was well related to the living and dining rooms but not to the garden, much of which was hidden around the corner of the house.

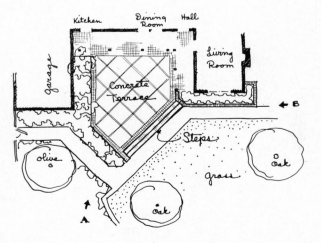

With the paving extended and the steps turned at a 45° angle, the terrace and garden flow together.

The eye is lazy and easily led.

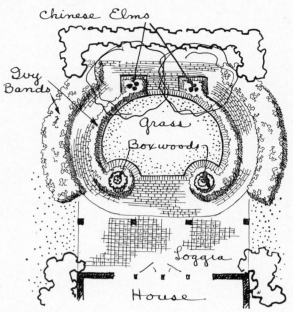

Chinese Elms

Ivy Bands

Grass

Boxwoods

Loggia

House

ALL BRICK

A grass panel becomes the terrace outside this garden room. Paths, mowing strips, and loggia paving are of brick. The boxwood and ivy are permanent and always green.

The multi-trunked trees lend an informal note to a symmetrical design.

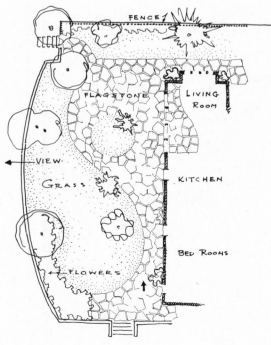

ALL FLAGSTONE

This large grass and flagstone terrace is easily accessible from most of the rooms of the house. Continuing the flagstone beyond the sliding glass doors makes a part of the living space into a garden room.

A woven sapling fence screens a neighbor's swimming pool.

Juniper, yew, and flowering dogwood keep the composition calm, permanent, and easy to care for.

MR. & MRS. WILLIAM BLACKIE, PEORIA, ILLINOIS 1949   ARCHITECT: CLETIS R. FOLEY

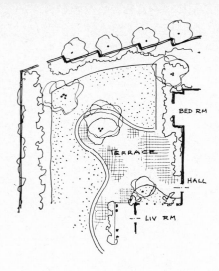

HIATT 1940

THERE ARE NO SET RULES FOR THE SHAPE OF A TERRACE, but its design must solve the problem set for it and be in good proportion to the house and the rest of the garden.

It may be curved, straight or angled, as long as there is a valid reason. If a rectangle seems the easiest, it could be the best.

One terrace may be curved to include a tree or a view, another may be angled to provide additional sitting space.

Arbitrary shapes—amoebas, zigzags, etc. used without reason or apparent forethought, can be disastrous and become constant irritants in the scheme.

BAXTER 1946

▶

The Stockstroms' house blends so gradually with its garden deck, situated among the trees, that it is hard to know where one ends and the other begins.

The living room opens onto a screened porch where the view is framed in a center panel of plate glass. The roof is extended farther to form an open porch.

The view up the river is a special asset, and the lines of the deck are turned to feature it.

A seat-high parapet, three feet wide, which serves as a place to sit or sun-bathe, or as a table for cocktails, magazines, and ash trays.

On the combined terrace-deck there's both sun and shade, and the choice of shelter or a breeze.

CLARK 1937

BOONE 1950

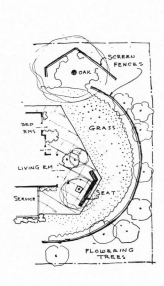

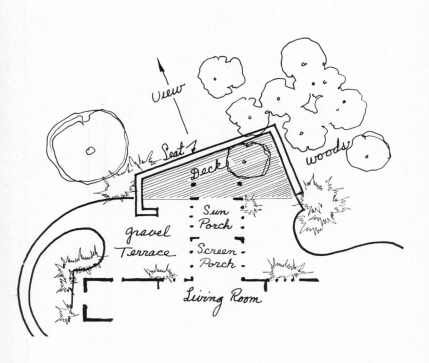

MR. & MRS. ARTHUR STOCKSTROM, ST. LOUIS, MISSOURI 1951

ARCHITECT: HARRIS ARMSTRONG　　　PHOTOGRAPHER: EZRA STOLLER

Trees already grown are invaluable. To have them, or not to have them is, to speak in a business phrase, to begin with capital or without it. *"The Doctor"—Robert Southey (1774–1843)*

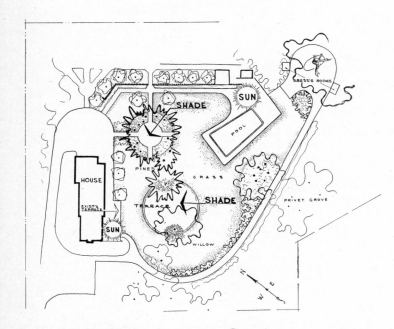

TAKE YOUR SHADE WHERE YOU FIND IT

Never underestimate the value of large trees already grown on the property—even if at first they seem to be in all the wrong places.

None of the big trees in this garden shaded the house or even its terraces . . . so a new terrace was created on an island in the lawn, where it would be shaded by the willows.

The owner wanted azaleas . . . azaleas need shade . . . so they were planted in a terrace under the pines.

Swimmers want sunshine . . . so the pool was placed in a clearing beyond the willows and given its own terrace.

The result is a somewhat casual plan with the various desired features grouped in the lawn area.

A swimming pool
on the main terrace

Some people prefer a pool in an area of its own, separate from the activities of the house.

Others want their pool right in the center of things so that all activities are together. There are, of course, certain advantages in entertaining, watching the children, serving food, and using the house facilities when the pool is near the house.

Many have a problem instead of a choice because of the size, topography, and orientation of their properties.

The Brookses' property was not large—it sloped, and the best exposure for the terrace and the pool was at the front of the house. A further complication was the need for screening from the driveway and street.

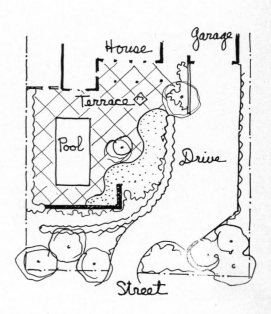

THE LATH HOUSE BEFORE IT WAS REMODELED

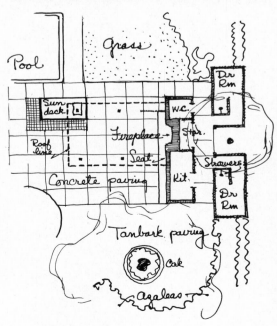

Pool
Grass
Dr Rm
Sun deck
W.C.
Fireplace
Stair.
Roof line
Seat
Drawers
Concrete paving
Kit.
Dr Rm
Tanbark paving
Oak
Azaleas

MR. & MRS. MERVIN G. ZELINSKY, ATHERTON 1947

PHOTOGRAPHER: JOHN ROBINSON

IF YOU REMODEL AN OLD GARDEN

Look carefully at all existing features before
the bulldozer moves in.

Trees, which you think must come out, may be
saved and pruned.

Outmoded outbuildings, walls, and old foundations, which at first glance seem to be
unwanted clutter, may have a definite use if
you design around them.

Old pergolas and arbors, which make you shudder,
can become assets when integrated with
a vigorous new conception.

The lath house, which the Zelinskys inherited
when they bought the property, was a
large solid block in the center of their proposed
pool and entertainment area. With the
sides removed, it is a light, airy structure around
which the whole scheme revolves.

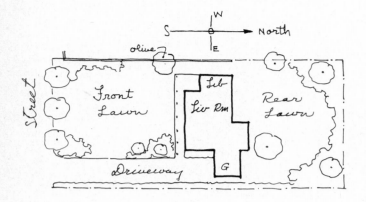

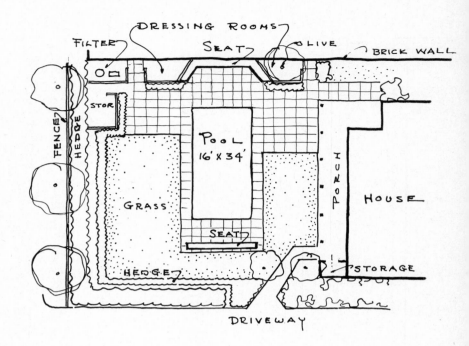

FOR PROPER ORIENTATION
THIS POOL IS
IN THE FRONT GARDEN

The rear garden at the Thieriots was too cold and too damp for a pool and its activities. It didn't take long to decide to use the sunny front garden for the pool and terrace.

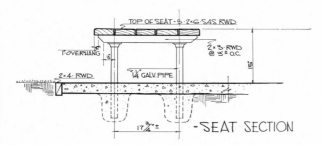

TOP OF SEAT · 5 · 2×6 · S4S RWD

1" OVERHANG

2×3 RWD
@ 3± O.C.

2×4 RWD

¼ GALV. PIPE

17 ¾ ±

— SEAT SECTION

Existing hedges and large chestnut trees gave immediate screening from the street.

Board and batten fencing along the neighbor's brick wall encloses open-air dressing rooms and space for storage and filter.

The concrete paving is ample for furniture and sun-pads. Paving is warm pinkish tan; cushions are grey.

The hedges are kept neatly trimmed, and large pots of bright pink geraniums provide color.

DESIGNED FOR

MINIMUM MAINTENANCE

Verna and Bill Jones wanted a lot of things on their small property.

Their list included:

> Parking for about five cars
> Privacy from the street
> Terraces off the living room and bedroom
> A small dipping pool near the bedroom
> Some flowers in raised beds
> Work area with more storage and a tool house
> Vegetables and cut flowers

They wanted it all neat and easy to keep in order.

The plan shows how they got everything they asked for.

Section shows handling of grades from neighbor's walnut trees to the Joneses' garden.

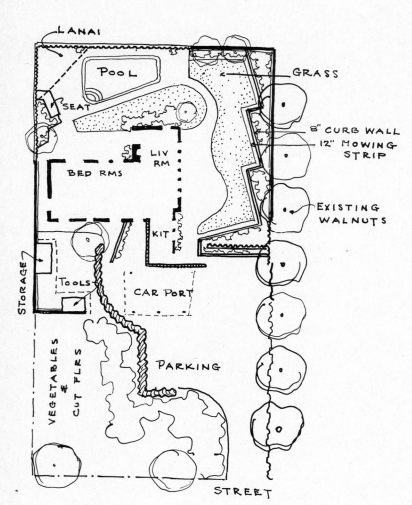

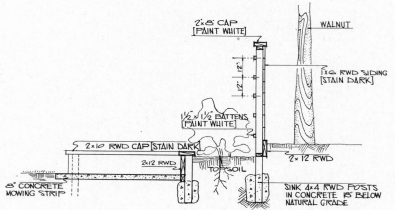

A boundary fence encloses the rear yard, giving privacy and a decorative background for the flowers in the raised beds.

The lawn is 3 inches below the terrace so it may be watered by flooding, a common practice in that area.

A 12-inch wide concrete mowing strip along the grass areas minimizes hand trimming.

The neighbor's walnut trees are a welcome background.

MORE ▶

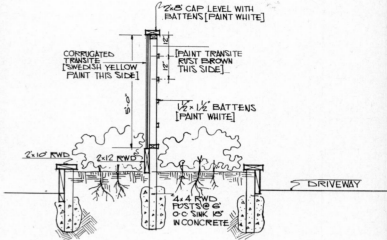

A baffle fence screens the garden from the entrance court.

See construction detail to the right.

This before picture, above, shows the original garden terrace open to the street.

Now the wall and the baffle fence of corrugated asbestos, which Bill Jones built himself, give complete privacy.

A POOL AND SUNSHADE ON A BEDROOM TERRACE

A triangular shaped roof, supported on pipe columns,
creates shade by the pool. An open section allows the breeze
to come through.

Paving is warm buff to reduce glare; corrugated
asbestos wall is painted bright yellow.

One side of the thirty-foot pool is on the diagonal to allow the
terrace to flow freely and to give a more spacious
feeling.

The wood bench is 42 inches wide for sun-bathing.

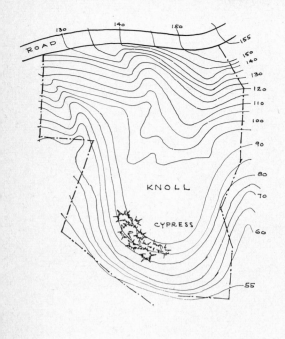

Before

There was a drop of 95 feet across the property and a flat knoll in the center, 40 feet below the road.

Roses and native plants are Mrs. Sperry's specialities. Her rose garden is incorporated in the terrace.

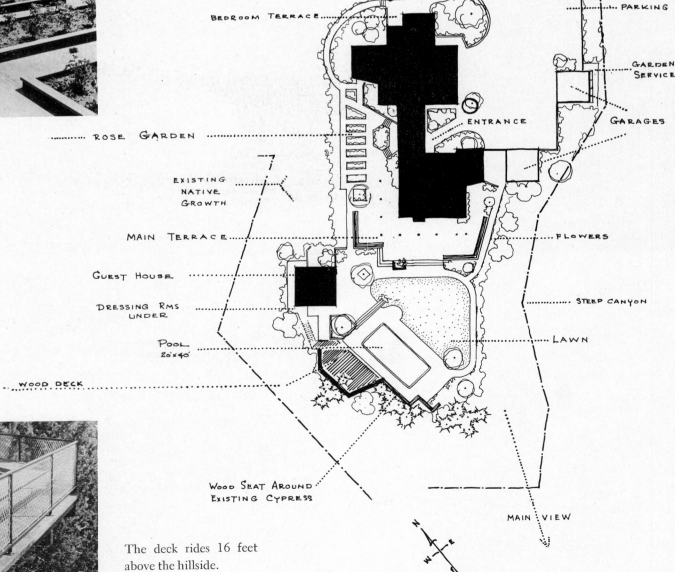

The deck rides 16 feet above the hillside.

After

A planting box for succulents interrupts the broad steps. Laundry tubs painted black hold pink geraniums.

IT WAS A RUGGED SITE

In some sections of the country, the most exciting and picturesque land for a building site is high property surrounded by hills and canyons.

The Sperrys owned a site so steep that—in view of their program— it was a temptation to advise them to sell it and look again.

But they were persistent, optimistic, and in love with the view and the native Ceanothus which covered the property.

Their architects agreed that the knoll should be used for the pool and garden and designed a house that steps down the hillside on three levels.

The two-story pavilion is a pool and guest house with dressing rooms for swimmers on the lower level.

A low, broad seat fits around the existing cypress at the end of the pool.

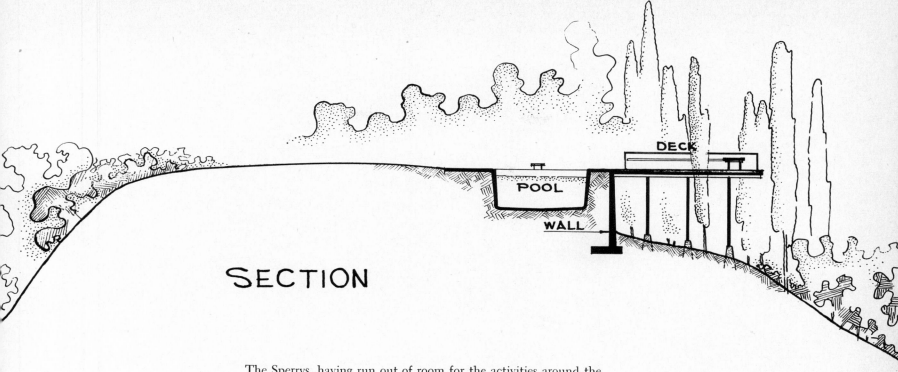

POOL

WALL

DECK

SECTION

The Sperrys, having run out of room for the activities around the pool, extended the level space by constructing a wood deck over the hillside.

The feeling of suspension in the landscape is exhilarating, and the view back to the house is rewarding.

No discussion of terraces is complete without reviewing the potentialities of the wood deck.

The examples on the following pages show how decks may supplement the available level areas in a garden.

Wood decks

in one form or another, have
been with us for a long time,
from the balconies of the Swiss chalets
to the spacious Victorian ve-
randas. Somewhere between 1890 and
1930 we lost the big porch,
the rocking chair, and the asparagus
fern; we also lost the carriage
and the parasol we used to watch go
by. The street, once tree-lined
and quiet except for the clip-clop of
horses and the children playing
drop-the-handkerchief on the lawn, is
now noisy, and the speed of
cars is tiring to the eye.

The Victorian seldom left his porch,
but now we live in *all* parts of
our domain and the old porch may
reappear far out under a tree
or in any part of the garden.

Landscape architecture is indispensable
for living the good life . . . it is for
human enjoyment in the 20th century
not for Sunday promenading in the
19th. *Gardens in the Modern Landscape"—Christopher Tunnard, 1938*

HAEFELIN GARDEN, PEORIA, ILLINOIS 1952

DECKS ANSWER OTHERWISE UNSOLVABLE PROBLEMS

Sometimes it's not possible to get level space by filling or by retaining walls, because you can't fill against wood houses or around trees or against the neighbor's fence. Decks are not inexpensive but may be the only way to get space where you want it.

The Haefelins wanted to serve directly from the kitchen to a terrace without going up and down steps.

Their deck-terrace at floor level solved the problem. It is a pleasant transition from the house to the garden.

The deck needed a wall to stop the afternoon wind. It's partially of glass to allow a view of the flower garden.

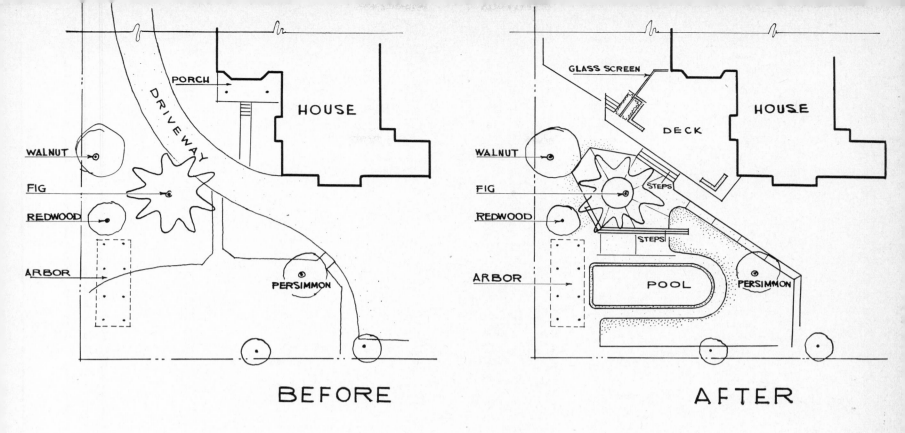

BEFORE

AFTER

Dr. Lucas bought an old but comfortable house and remodeled it.

The garden was three feet below the house level and was divided by an old-fashioned driveway which encircled the house.

A solid terrace was impractical because of wooden foundations and areaways for basement windows. The deck which was added has a fireplace and is big enough for large parties.

Wide wood steps lead to a lower level (determined by the old fig tree) and then on down more broad wood steps to the swimming pool. The old wisteria-covered arbor in the original garden now shades one end of the pool.

Entrance and driveway were combined on the other side of the house.

A DECK SOLVES A
GRADE PROBLEM

The Sterns, wanting a terrace on the same level as the new addition to the house and not daring to risk filling on the tree, built this wood deck-terrace.

MR. & MRS. CARL W. STERN, ATHERTON 1951

124   ARCHITECT: GERMANO MILONO   LANDSCAPE CONTRACTOR: OUTDOOR CONSTRUCTION, INC.

A DECK SOLVES A

MAINTENANCE PROBLEM

The bottom of the garden was a catch-all in plain view from the library. Now it's pleasant to look at and invites you into the garden.

BEFORE

This deck becomes a tree house built in the upper branches of a group of live oaks.

A shaded terrace for the Fahrneys, it commands their best view of San Francisco Bay.

MR. & MRS. PAUL L. FAHRNEY, KENT WOODLANDS 1950   **PHOTOGRAPHER: MAYNARD PARKER**

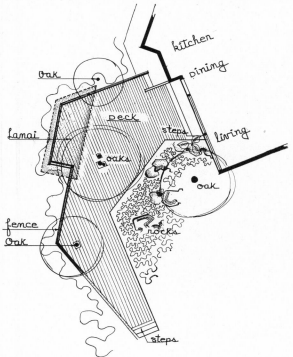

The problem of projecting yourself into a natural landscape without destroying it is solved here by a large deck-platform.

The natural rocks, native plants, and live oaks all remain untouched. A shelter and a fence to screen the road are at deck level.

MISS ALICE ERVING, SANTA BARBARA
ARCHITECTS: LUTAH MARIA RIGGS & ARVIN B. SHAW, III   PHOTOGRAPHER: MAYNARD PARKER   127

The sea washes up many things.
This old log appeared on
the Benoists' doorstep one morning after a storm.

CHAPTER FIVE

Beach gardens

The usual cottage at the beach is small, compact, and
inexpensive. Used mainly for week ends,
it is informal, and the main activities are swimming, eating, and sun-bathing. There is very little
gardening—in fact, the plants must endure long stretches
of neglect, and ground covers and native beach
grasses should cover large areas.

The next three gardens are from a group at Aptos Beach, near
Monterey. They are windswept, so each garden has its
own private and sheltered sand for sun-bathing.

No concrete paving was used because the weight of masonry seems
out of place with sand and water; besides, wood is more
comfortable to walk on and weathers beautifully in the salt air.

BEFORE

MR. & MRS. CHARLES O. MARTIN, APTOS 1948

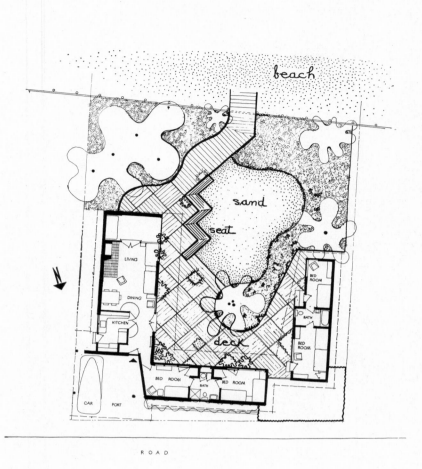

The Martins moved several old shacks together for the bedrooms and built a new living room and garden.

It sleeps, feeds, and sunbathes eight people with little effort.

The lines of the garden are restless and flowing, like the sea.

All rooms open on the deck, which looks out to sea.

The dining terrace and the sandbox have wind protection on the lower level.

The seats are wide enough for mattresses. Planting is simple—pines, ice plant, and a few marguerites for color.

This nondescript house was moved from another site and set on a new foundation. A coat of paint and a gay awning gave it a new personality.

DECK, SAND AND
SUCCULENTS

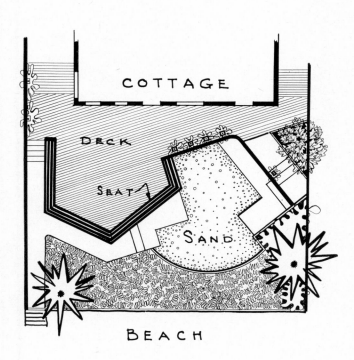

The sand area is below the garden level for protection from the wind.

Screen fences give privacy without interfering with the neighbors' view.

A GARDEN ON A LAGOON

Belvedere lagoon is man-made, with many peninsulas, and every owner has a waterfront lot. Controlled by floodgates, the water is kept at a constant level.

These people have sun, deck space, sailing and swimming, ample room for gardening, and distant views.

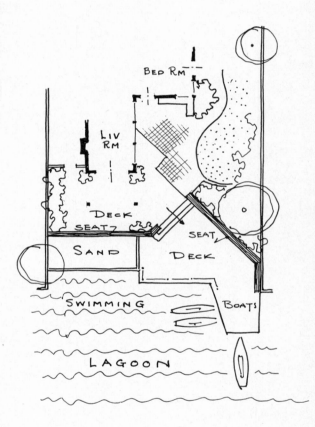

A GARDEN ON A SOUND

The traditional method of locating a house along this beach is to bulldoze a level area and push the house into the dune.

The scheme shown here features the dune and preserves its graceful lines by making the house and deck appear to float over it.

With the second floor several feet higher than the dune, the drama of the site is retained and the eye is carried to the horizon with a minimum of interference.

The cantilevered deck foreshortens the public beach below, giving complete privacy to the living room.

MR. & MRS. GEORGE MAREK, FIRE ISLAND, N. Y. 1950

ARCHITECT: ELDREDGE SNYDER   PHOTOGRAPHER: MAYNARD PARKER   137

MRS. CLINTON S. WALKER, CARMEL 1953

A GARDEN BY THE SEA

The house, of native Carmel stone, is built on a rocky headland.

Driftwood, washed up by the sea, is the sculptural interest.

Shells, succulents, and seaweed decorate the garden.

ARCHITECT: FRANK LLOYD WRIGHT   LANDSCAPE CONTRACTOR: ALF NILSSEN   139

CHAPTER SIX

Remodeling

Millions of homes throughout the country are in various stages of obsolescence. This is particularly true in cities as families move farther out into the thousands of tract houses offering them suburban living.

Many of the old houses left behind will be torn down—others will be remodeled by people who want to stay in town and who can't face the cost of city land and new construction.

Be careful, or you'll find you can't face the cost of remodeling, either. Before you get too enthusiastic, get the advice of an architect and a builder. Perhaps the old house can't be revived to last another generation; but if the style interests you and the arrangement suits you and you get the green light, start to dream. Partitions can be moved and additions made. Decks and porches can be added, and the garden space developed.

You will find that old trees, outbuildings, masses of stone rubble, old foundations, and arbors will be very usable in reconstructing the garden.

The wrecker and the second-hand material firms will become your friends.

You will discover all about dry-rot, termites, and what the Revised City Code says about exposed wiring and the proper venting of gas heaters.

While there is terrific excitement and convenience in living in a modern house, there is also a particular kind of serenity that comes with age—a nostalgic quality in a style that is content to sit on a side street.

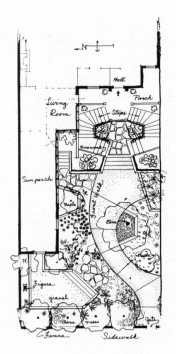

The past is not for burning.—*John Yeon, in a letter to* House Beautiful, *1952*

The people who remodeled this house liked its style and location. They enjoy adding to its collection of Victorian architectural trivia and enjoy installing the latest conveniences behind its mouldings and panels.

Built in 1862, it was ready to be torn down by 1933 when they first moved in. Minor repairs and a bathroom sufficed until the depression was over. Remodeled many times during the past twenty years, it now appears as you see it (opposite page) after replacing the old entrance steps with a double stairway and adding a new garden.

1934

saw the garden in a
formal pattern
with tables, chairs, pea-
cocks, and globes
of clipped boxwood. A
sloping board
fence protected the gar-
den from the
street. Sycamores were
planted as a
screen, and a dog-run
added along
the side property.

1948

found the formality softened by
the exuberance of plant
growth. The fence is higher and
level, with ivy trained in
a diamond pattern. The dog-run
has been replaced by a
new wing on the house and elms
planted along the entrance
path.

1954

After twenty years, there were too many
plants and too many trees and major
changes were indicated.

The entrance walk now curves to meet the
new stairs and the planting is
completely informal.

The color picture (opposite) was taken in
August, when the summer color
was at its height. In December (below) the
flowers are gone, but there is sufficient pattern in the freer layout to carry
the interest throughout the winter.

The Richmonds had an old house in a built-up neighborhood.

There was a garage in the middle of the lot because at
that time they didn't know where to put it except where the
stable used to be.

Various owners had spent years trying to plant out this building.
only to make it more and more of an obstruction.
Now, cleared of all planting, it looks like a vine-covered cottage in the garden and seems at home.

Clipping nearly 400 feet of privet hedge was a lot of work. Wood
fences were substituted, which resulted in about six
more feet of over-all width in the garden.

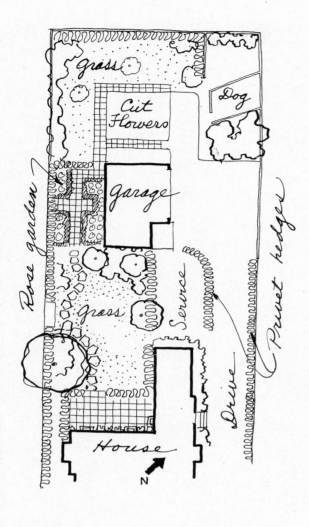

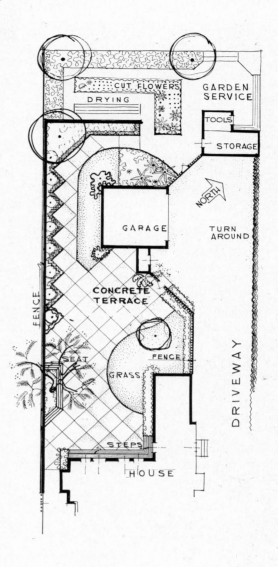

Before

A small terrace crowded into the shade, a large lawn

Service area took up valuable space, surrounded by thick privet hedges. Garage and driveway cramped

Boxwood and rose garden stopped vista, seemed crowded between garage and property hedge

Privet hedges on property line and around the service area used up valuable space on a narrow lot, clipping took too much time

After

A large terrace with sun and shade, a small lawn

Service moved to unused area at rear, includes storage and tool house, driveway widened

Some boxwood and roses moved into new pattern, vista carries around garage

Fences, used for vines and roses, substitute for 75% of the former hedge

REMODELING

CITY GARDENS

"You go out through the cellar door—"

YEARS AGO, little consideration was given to the relationship between the house and its plot of ground.

If people wanted sunshine, they had a conservatory filled with Boston ferns, colored glass, and aspidistras.

If the children needed an airing, they were taken around the block.

Eating outside was called a picnic, and they went to the park.

If they wanted a view, they sat on the front veranda.

BEFORE

TODAY, when you remodel, you may have to contrive new ways to get from the house to the garden.

You'll find yourself changing windows to doors and solid walls to glass.

You'll build decks out over cellar windows, bridges from second-story rooms, and wide inviting steps into a new and more usable garden.

You'll create small and easily maintained plots to garden in and large and convenient areas to live in.
You'll turn old woodsheds into garden houses and old garden houses into woodsheds.

It's fun, and you'll enjoy it.

HENRIETTA MOFFAT GARDEN, SAN FRANCISCO

The Sintons, who bought an old house, were faced with the problem of remodeling it or tearing it down and starting over. The house was sound and the location good, so they decided to remodel.

A floating stairway leads from a balcony off the dining room to the garden.

HENRY SINTON GARDEN, SAN FRANCISCO

ARCHITECTS: CLARK & BUETTLER
PHOTOGRAPHER: MAYNARD PARKER

CHARLES FIELD GARDEN, SAN FRANCISCO
ARCHITECTS: WEIHE, FRICK AND KRUSE

The Fields remodeled an old shingle house which had turned its back on the small garden (30′ x 36′).

The bay windows in the dining room were changed to French doors, and a deck at floor level was extended over to the kitchen and out into the garden.

It's convenient, it's sunny, and it's secluded.

147

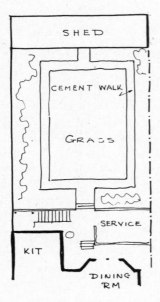

The Kirkhams changed a typical
back yard with a southern exposure into an
area which they, their children, and
their guests use constantly.

The original garden, a story below the dining room, was a square plot with an
old shed across the rear of the property.

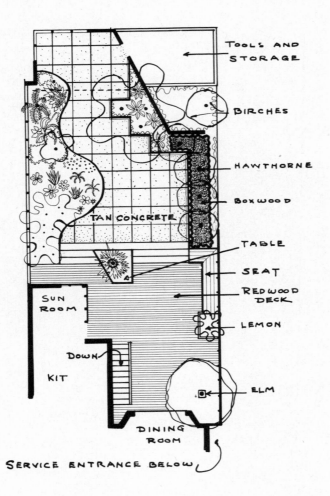

The garden now seems twice as big because the static lines of the
original rectangle have been changed. The moving lines
of the curve play against the angular forms on the opposite side.

Half of the old shed was converted into a summer house and
the rest left for tools and storage.

A trellis fence, built against the neighbor's concrete wall, gives
a sense of enclosure and structural continuity.

MORE ▶

LANDSCAPE CONTRACTOR: BERNARD GAYMAN

PHOTOGRAPHER: RONDAL PARTRIDGE

BEFORE

The dining room windows are at the far left, the back porch at the right.

REVIVING A BACK YARD

A wood deck, complete with built-in seats, tables, and planting pockets, was built at the dining room level and connects with the old back porch for serving from the kitchen. French doors open onto the deck from the dining room; the fence along the side increases privacy.

Space for service deliveries and garbage cans is under the deck.

In the naïve days of the old brownstone fronts, when, even if there was no daylight saving, the hours were less crowded and one could easily reach the country, the space back of these houses was given over to a wilderness of clothes-lines, ashcans and prowling tomcats. It was veiled from sight by the thick draperies of the period and seen only by the servants and the iceman. *"Your City Garden"—Margaret McKenney and E. L. D. Seymour, 1937*

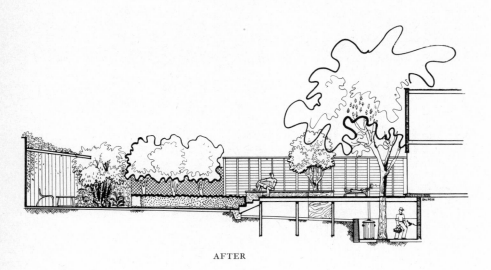

NEIGHBOR'S HOUSE ↓

BEFORE

AFTER

The garden is now level, private, and accessible.

An elm tree comes up through the deck
and will provide shade
and an additional screen.

Paving is pebble concrete, with a 2″ x 4″ redwood
pattern of 6-foot squares.

The fences, of wood and corrugated asbestos, are painted yellow
with white trim.

Cacti and succulents predominate in the planting.

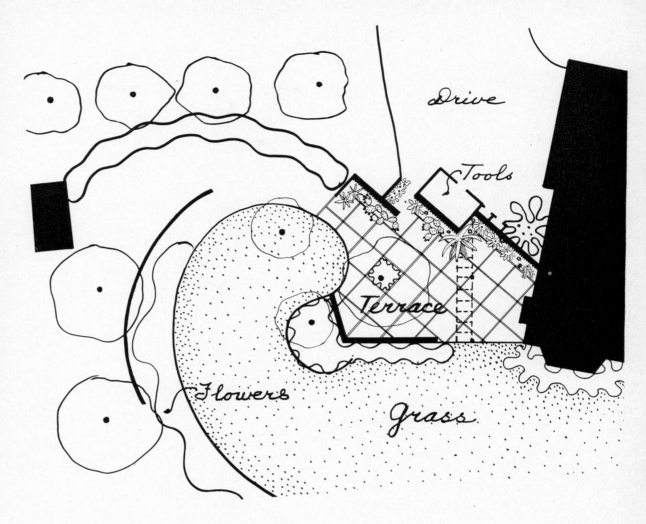

Often it is practical or desirable not to do an extensive remodeling of a garden but only to solve a specific problem in one area.

The Wildmans' most pressing problem was for some shelter over the French doors of the living room, which faced west. Just outside was a formal rose garden, but what they really wanted there was an informal terrace for entertaining.

The splayed fence lines and diagonal paving pattern increase the apparent size of the garden.

MORE ▶

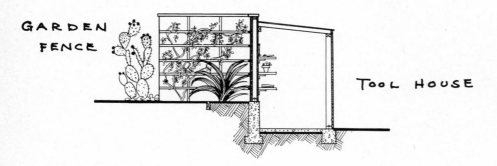

GARDEN
FENCE

TOOL HOUSE

Giant bamboo is used as a background for
the new terrace.

A tool house and potting bench are built
as a lean-to on the driveway side
of the fence.

Both the structural materials and plants
have been chosen to create definite
shadow patterns.

In a garden scene . . .
although this is a mat-
ter very little con-
sidered, an immense
deal of the beauty will
depend upon the nice
arrangement of parts to
secure light and shade.
"Landscape Gardening"
—*Kemp, 1850*

THE CARPENTERS REMODELED
THEIR DOUBLE GARAGE

Their suburban back yard (30′ x 50′) was domi-
nated by a two-car garage (which they didn't
need) and had no direct access from the living room (which they wanted).

The other things they wanted were:

A place to sit and a place to eat outdoors
Play space for the children
Storage area and a potting bench
Drying yard and work space
Wood storage
Some flower beds

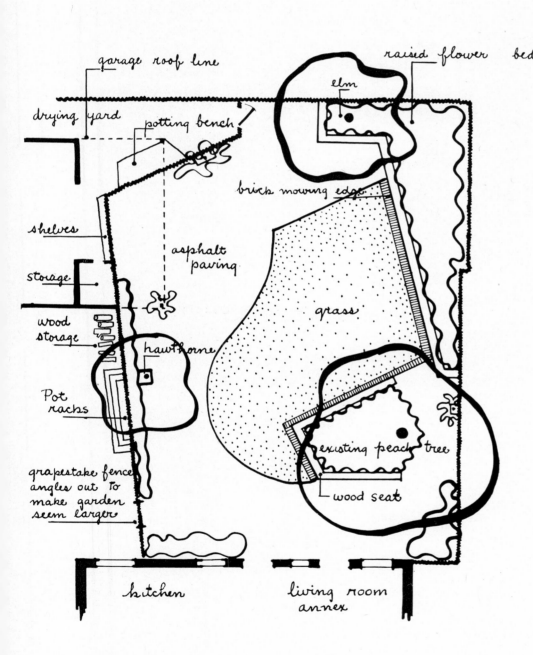

If you're a one-car family with a two-car garage,
chances are the extra space fills up with
miscellaneous items which soon become inacces-
sible, disorganized, and untidy.

If the garage is in the back yard and con-
fronts you with its uncompromising rectangle,
consider turning it into a garden sum-
merhouse as the Carpenters did.

MORE ▶

Removing two sides of the garage and extending the garden fence under the roof line were the only changes needed to create a small but very usable summer house.

The paved area is large enough for a picnic table and a portable barbecue.

The grapestake fence, at an angle, makes the space seem larger and forms the back wall of a storage closet and potting bench.

MR. & MRS. THOMAS P. CARPENTER

The raised flower bed along the property fence is seat-high. When the children grow up, the sandbox under the tree will become a flower bed.

The house has been remodeled to permit access to the garden without going through the kitchen.

In the decorations, however, of grounds adjoining a house, much should depend upon the character of the house itself. . . . *"An Analytical Enquiry into the Principles of Taste"*— *Richard Payne Knight, 1805*

The Cartans needed a garden shelter with dressing rooms for the swimmers, but they also needed the existing garage at the back of the garden.

The summer house, designed to harmonize with the old Victorian dwelling, was built against the back wall of the garage. It has a fireplace, and there's a bar and room for storage behind the old-fashioned shutter doors.

"WE BOUGHT

AN OLD

FARMHOUSE . . ."

It's never safe to show "before" pictures of old farmhouses; they're nostalgic and photogenic and invariably have more charm than the "after" pictures.

But to photograph them and to live in them are two different things.

Not wanting to change the original house any more than necessary, the Griffins added only a large deck at floor level, with wide front steps, and provided a play space for the children and room for a barbecue. A generous parking area completed their needs for easy country living.

A wisteria, planted many years ago at the corner of the house, was saved to grow through a space left for it in the new deck.

BEFORE

MR. & MRS. EVERETT GRIFFIN, SANTA CRUZ 1950

BEFORE

A ranch house, built many years ago, has been restored to become a year-round residence.

Below, this view of the entrance shows the generous parking area.

MR. & MRS. HANNES SCHROLL, MAYFIELD 1946

A sixty-foot terrace reaches out from the shade of the bay tree for sunshine and a view of the pool.

It is spacious enough to hold comfortable chairs, dining tables, umbrellas, and potted plants without seeming crowded.

BEFORE

Rambling, old-fashioned gardens, with no apparent plan, that have just grown through the years, can have a very special charm. But the success of such a garden depends on the plants rather than on the design and structural materials. To be a joy forever, the plants must first be carefully chosen and even more carefully tended.

BEFORE

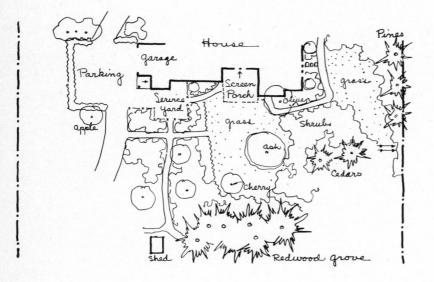

The garden the Murphys acquired had once been like that, but several years of neglect had done it in.

Its face might have been lifted if they had wanted to devote a lot of time to it; but for Mrs. Murphy it was too shady, too closed in, and too far gone.

"I'm being smothered," said Mrs. Murphy. "Tear off the old porch, take out the redwoods, *do something*."

AFTER

The porch came off and twenty-two truckloads of overgrown shrubbery were hauled away.

The screened porch became a terrace-lanai, closely related to the garden.

A guava, a persimmon, and a weeping cherry, lost in the overgrowth, were saved and are specimens in the new garden.

MORE ▶

THE NEW CARPORT

The Murphys' complaints were specific and valid:
1. Claustrophobia
2. The garage was several feet too short for their cars
3. The parking area was much too small
4. The screened porch had been added with an obvious disregard for the pleasant Mediterranean style of the house
5. The thick grove of redwoods was oppressive and blocked out the afternoon sunshine
6. There was no terrace in the sun

THE OLD GARAGE

The old garage was given over to garden tools and much-needed storage.

A new carport for three automobiles was built as an ell to the house. This addition provided wind protection and privacy for the new terrace.

The driveway was widened and the parking area tripled, resulting in greater convenience and reduced maintenance.

The redwood grove was kept but pruned high to let sunshine filter in. Golden bamboo was planted beyond to pick up the late sun and brighten the background.

The tanbark circle under the trees is defined by a low wood curb stained brown.

ADDING A NEW CARPORT, SUN PORCH, AND TERRACE

MADE THIS OLD HOUSE FUNCTION FOR THE NEW OWNER

The ash tree in the center of the lawn was handsome but neglected. Pruned to let in the sunlight, sprayed and fed, it frames the lanai when seen from the redwood circle.

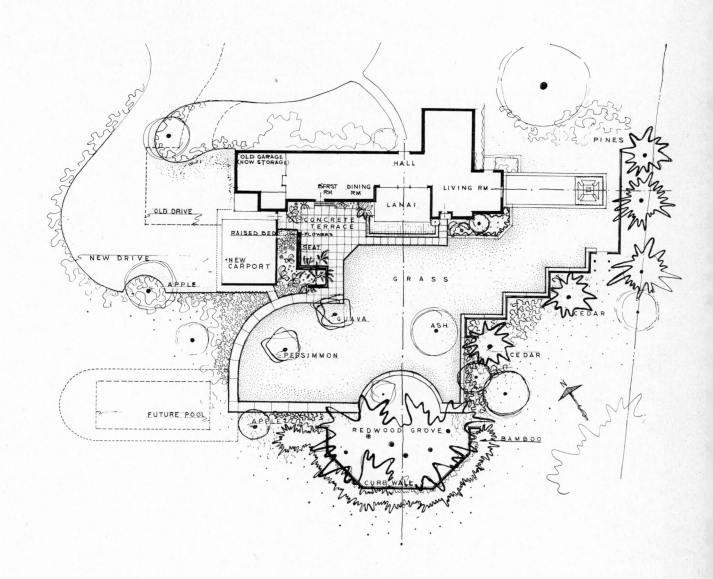

THE OLD GARDEN

REMODELING OLD GARDENS

The existing layout of an old garden is seldom just right for
the new owners. Times change, requirements change,
and tastes change from one generation to another and from
one family to another.

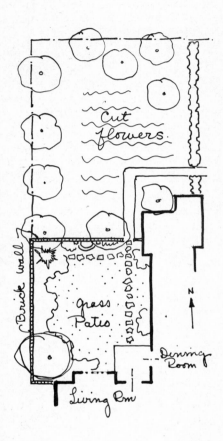

THE NEW GARDEN

The Witters acquired a well-designed traditional French
house. Off the main rooms was an enclosed garden
with a latticed wall. It could have been revived and made into
a charming court for someone who wanted an enclosed
garden with a latticed wall, but Mrs. Witter wanted to walk
out into her flower garden, wanted to see the rest
of the property and trees, and wanted the whole thing to be
more free and easy.

Removing most of the wall resulted in a longer vista and a
more intimate view of the trees along the property line.

Cut flower gardens are attractive, but the effect is seldom
permanent enough to be the main view from a terrace.
To see and not to see was solved by building baffle fences,
which screen the cutting garden from the house terrace
but let it unfold gradually as you walk down
the garden path.

The espaliers are star jasmine and loquat.

The concrete paving is
finished to expose
the black pebble aggre-
gate; 2″ x 4″ red-
wood strips make a pat-
tern of 3-foot
squares.

View from the terrace

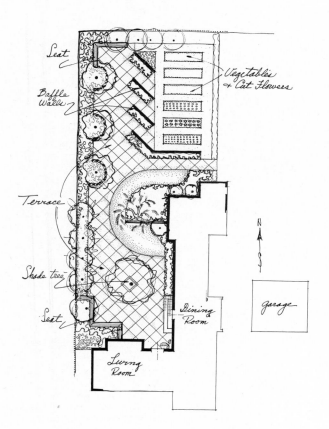

View toward the house showing how the baffles relate to the cutting garden.

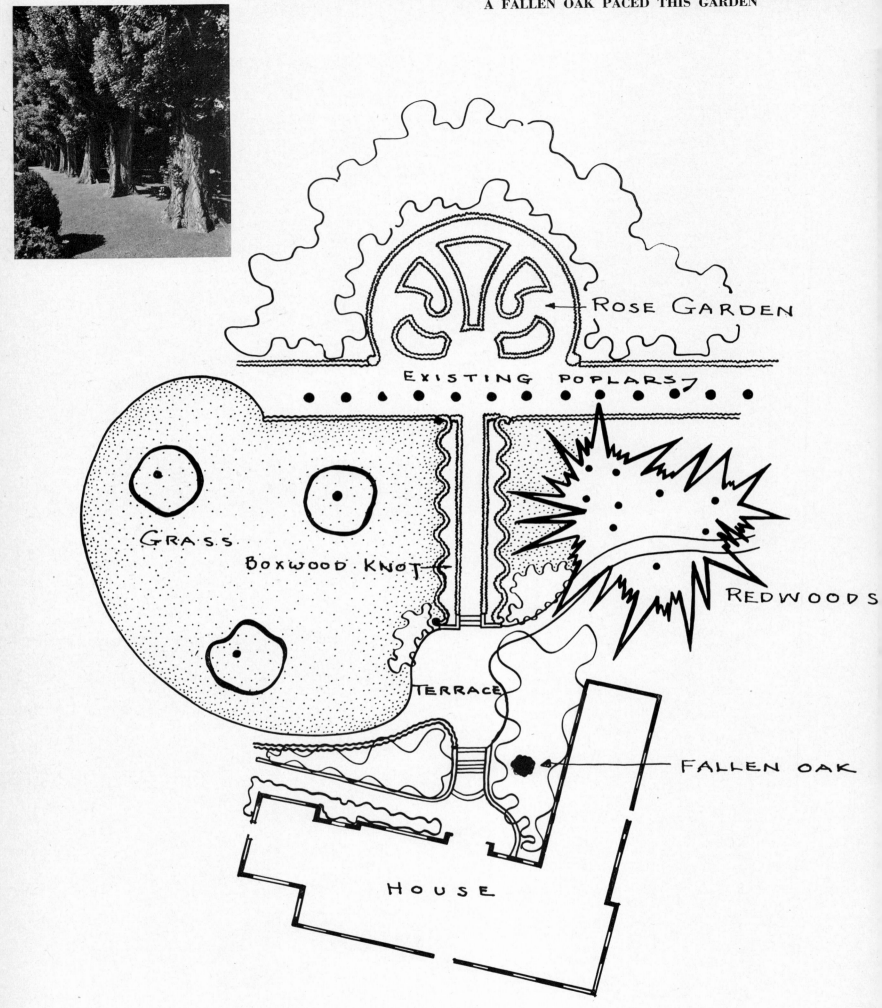

ROSE GARDEN

EXISTING POPLARS

GRASS

BOXWOOD KNOT

REDWOODS

TERRACE

FALLEN OAK

HOUSE

MR. & MRS. BENJAMIN C. KEATOR

STONE MASON: ANGELO ANTONIAZZI

Just outside the entrance hall door was a large fallen live oak, still growing and in good condition, but nearly hidden by shrubbery. One large branch arched over a potential vista; another rested just two feet from the ground. Stone steps were built up and over this branch, which itself formed the top step.

MORE ▶

The oak is festooned with variegated ivy and hung with baskets of fuchsias and begonias.

The central path extends to a row of magnificent old Lombardy poplars. Beyond lies a boxwood parterre planted with seasonal annuals— nemesia in the spring, stock in the summer, Mexican zinnias in the fall, and white begonias in the winter.

MR. & MRS. BENJAMIN C. KEATOR, HILLSBOROUGH 1941   PHOTOGRAPHER: PHILIP FEIN

A DRIVEWAY FROM THE CARRIAGE

DAYS IS RESTUDIED

The Earls have a remodeled garden. The old driveway went all around the house; it cut up the lawn, crossed the south façade, and exposed the garage to view from the main rooms of the house.

A new parking and arrival court at the front of the house allowed them to abandon the circular drive.

The south garden now has a 70-foot terrace, an oak-studded lawn, and a flower border against the grapestake fence.

◀

The Keators had an informal overgrown garden with boxwood-bordered flower beds along its wandering paths.

The boxwood was used to make this knot garden along the new path and to border the rose garden beds in the distance.

MORE ▶

MR. & MRS. AUSTIN W. EARL

LANDSCAPE CONTRACTORS: HUETTIG & SCHROMM   PHOTOGRAPHER: RONDAL PARTRIDGE   171

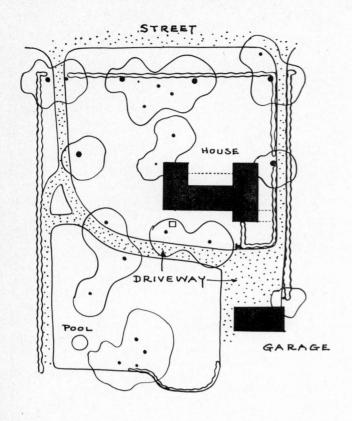

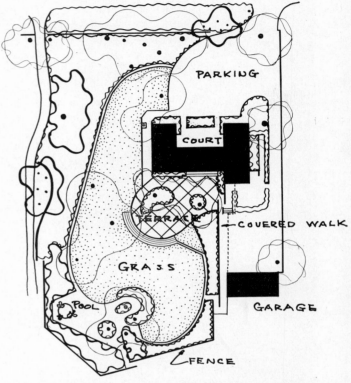

MR. & MRS. AUSTIN W. EARL

Large white oaks within the bounds of the new terrace cast winter shadows on the paving.

The wood fence, with ivy in a diamond pattern, screens the covered walk between the garage and the house.

The wide curved steps are low and comfortable. (Risers are 4 inches, treads 18 inches.)

The terrace is pebble concrete, divided by redwood headers into 10-foot squares.

CHAPTER SEVEN

Garden

What are the important details, and what structural materials are available to enrich the design of a garden?

Even with a good plan, the success of the garden will depend upon

> the intelligent placing, spacing, and interrelationship of the various elements
>
> understanding the possibilities and limits of structural and plant materials
>
> discreetly evaluating the weakness and strength of various colors and textures
>
> choosing materials which are sympathetic with the site, with each other, and with the people who are to see and use them.

There is no artificiality where there is no attempt to disguise materials. *"Art and Ornament"—Tunnard*

CORBUS GARDEN, MENLO PARK

details

TODAY'S SMALL GARDEN

with its avowed purpose of providing convenient pleasures and pleasant conveniences will need some or all of the following:

Retaining walls—when the bulldozer leaves the property looking as if it had been hit by a block-buster

Steps—for lots too steep for ramps; or for flat lots where differences in elevation are artificially created to add interest

Fences and walls—for protection and privacy

Paving—for terraces, walks, and service areas to avoid mud-tracking and to reduce maintenance

Play space for children—where they will be safe, contented, and easily watched

Built-in seating—to save moving too much furniture too often

Storage walls—to take the overflow

Raised flower and vegetable beds—for neatness and convenience

Mowing strips—to define lawn and planting areas and to simplify grass cutting

Service yards—no home is complete without one

Garden work area—for tools, incinerators, potting bench, mulch bin, *ad infinitum*

Pools—swimming, dipping, wading, fish, and lily

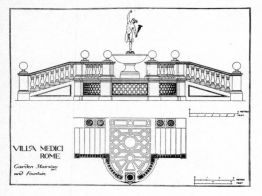

VILLA MEDICI

MENTON

GÖTEBORG

Steps

ROME

STEPS ARE FOR PEOPLE

The primary function of steps is to get from one level to another.

However, their possibilities as an important factor in design have been apparent throughout all the ages of building.

Their shape, extent, and material may be influenced by the absolute scale of the over-all composition, but their final allegiance is to the people who use them; and in detail they must never fail to relate to the scale of the human figure.

SAN
GIMIGNANO

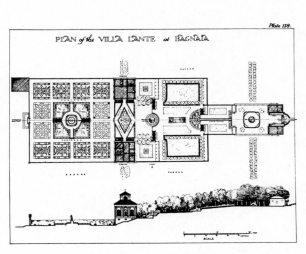

VILLA LANTE, BAGNAIA

CHICHICASTENANGO

SIENA

Designers use steps

in their compositions to produce emotion, to be a visual and an actual welcome into their designs, to form strong and dynamic horizontal lines across their buildings. Their scale, shape, direction, material, and decoration are subject to infinite variety, limited only by the designer's imagination.

In the great renaissance of gardening in Italy, designers were often faced with steep and difficult sites, where great ingenuity was required to relate one level to another. Their ramps and stairways often incorporated pools and fountains, highly embellished with ornament and sculpture.

While few of us want, or can have, our steps done in the grand manner, we can learn a great deal by studying these early examples. Their scale, flow of line, and dramatic quality have never been equaled.

VILLA D'ESTE, TIVOLI

RHEEM GARDEN, ORINDA

MILBANK GARDEN, PEBBLE BEACH

EARL GARDEN, ATHERTON

STEPS ARE FOR DESIGN

Steps can be much more than a connection between two levels.

They can have strength and crispness of line. They can steady the composition, point the direction, and ornament the scene.

Steps may be used to express the mood and tempo of the garden. They can put you in a leisurely mood, make you hurry, or arouse your curiosity.

Use them with care and forethought.

MENUHIN GARDEN, ALMA 1941

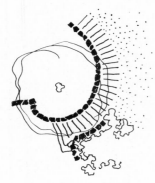

STEPS ARE FOR STEEP SITES

A long flight of steps on a steep site can be more important than
you intend. Too much masonry—too many re-
taining walls, landings, stepped cheek walls—can overpower all the other elements in the garden.

The steps above overcome a difference in elevation of fourteen
feet, yet they remain calm as they wind down around the
tree. With the stone wall only along one side, they descend the
hill quietly. Risers are 7 inches, treads 12 inches.

STEPS

ARE

FOR

ACCENT

AND

SHADOW

The size of a flight of steps will be influenced by its use as well as by the distance between the levels and their importance to the whole design.

Two people need 5 feet in width to walk comfortably down a flight of steps together.

Steps can be narrow and increase the visual separation of two levels—or they can be broad and make two separate areas seem as one.

GREENWOOD GARDEN, LAFAYETTE 1948

Steps are an invitation particularly if they're wide and comfortable.

Properly designed and located, they are one of the main devices by which the observer is enticed into the garden.

Steps should be placed so they may be used without constantly crossing conversation groups or quiet garden areas.

The curved terrace line, above, flows to wide steps that invite you to explore the upper garden.

181

Here, in a very formal plan, plants make an overlay of foliage and color. The strength of the garden lines is softened but not lost.

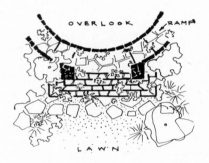

STEPS ARE FOR PLANTS

Nothing pleases the average gardener more than to soften the lines of steps with the informality of plants, whether they're grown beside, over, or in the steps.

Nurseries grow a great variety of dwarf perennials, alpines, and ground covers suitable for this kind of planting.

For best results, construct the pockets and plant as the steps are built. If the pockets are well drained, the plants will last for years.

These brick steps are softened by the irregular growth of juniper along the sides.

BRADLEY GARDEN, HILLSBOROUGH

ERVING GARDEN, SANTA BARBARA

Wood steps are fitted to the natural boulders. The paving is asphalt.

STONE AND WOOD

COMBINE TO MAKE

STEPS

FAHRNEY GARDEN, KENT WOODLANDS

Wood steps, made of 3″ x 6″ redwood planks, with open risers, wind up a rocky hill.

Brick step details

THE RISER AND TREAD RELATIONSHIP

makes or breaks the success of your steps. Don't think you're making it easier by making them lower. If you hear that 6-inch risers and 14-inch treads make a comfortable garden step (correct) don't try to make it still easier by reducing the riser to 4 inches unless you change the tread width as well. You'll probably turn your ankle.

There are few rules that can't be broken with delightful results, but this is one to respect:

> *Twice the riser plus the tread equals twenty-six inches.*

So if you want a 4-inch riser, you need an 18-inch tread.

All steps should have ⅛ inch to ¼ inch pitch (included in the riser dimension) to shed water.

If, to make the grade, you have to use an 8-inch riser, use a 10-inch tread. That's the old cellar step.

At a recent Cotillion, thirteen out of sixteen debutantes tripped into the arms of their escorts as they descended the stairs. It was found that the steps had 5-inch risers and 12-inch treads (5 inches + 5 inches + 12 inches = 22 inches). They had been made "low" to make it easy for the girls to "glide down gracefully." If the risers had been 5 inches and the treads 16 inches, the girls could have floated down as if on a cloud.

Brick steps with wood

Brick steps with brick

Wood steps with brick

BRICK

Brick is a sympathetic material, with the added advantage of being pre-cut in a size that's easy to handle and that lends itself to step dimensions.

Bricks range in color from the pale buff of Mexican brick through pinks and oranges to deep reds.

The color of the joints may be varied from pure white through natural and buff by adding pigment to the mortar.

Don't try to make the joints match the brick, it's disastrous.

Redwood bark

1" x 1" redwood

Open frame

Wood frame and wire

Grapestakes

Building lath

Terrace and boundary fence on a California tract house by Eichler Homes. The lot is 60' x 100'.

Fences

YOU MAY YEARN FOR THE GOOD OLD DAYS when lawns ran together and houses seemed spotted around in a little park.

Today's economic pressures dictate that houses in our subdivisions be built only a few feet apart—in endless monotony.

Natural foliage disappears with the grading; too much sun pours into the living room, bedrooms, or kitchen; the neighbor's radio pours in through the windows, and his children pull up your young corn.

You decide you must put up a fence. But what kind? The house material, other fences in the neighborhood, your personal likes and dislikes, and your budget will all influence your choice.

Wire and wood fences are least expensive and easiest to build. Wood lends itself to the greatest variety of patterns, combinations, and colors. The amateur carpenter-owner can install a good-looking fence himself on week ends.

Be sensible—realize that although the fence can be an important asset to the garden, it shouldn't dominate its surroundings. Too elaborate a combination of squares, triangles, or free forms or too many bright colors may overpower not only the garden but the Matisse in the living room.

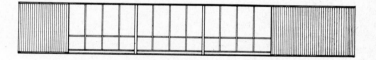

Frame of 4″ x 4″ posts on 8-foot centers with 2″ x 4″ uprights evenly spaced. Background of 1″ x 8″ shiplap siding is stained dark.

White fence frame with grey horizontal boards

THERE'S NO RIGHT OR WRONG SIDE
TO A FENCE ANY MORE

The "backside" of a wood fence has disappeared. The post and frame, which used to be turned away or covered with siding, has become a potential design factor.

A fence can be kept plain or made exciting, depending on the mood of the garden.

It can be used to create definite patterns and strong shadows.

It can be dark, to make it recede; or light, to bring it forward.

It can be solid, for complete privacy, partially open or louvered to appear light and airy, or mostly open to suggest boundary without being a barrier.

It can be straight, curved, baffled, or zigzagged to become a part of the general garden design.

Watch that you don't zig when you should zag. The rule is—when in doubt, don't.

Frame of fence grey with weathered boards

The tasteful forms in which iron fences are made, together with their indestructible character, will continue to make them more and more desirable. *"Suburban Home Grounds"*— *F. J. Scott, 1870*

Egg-crate frame in sun shows strong shadow pattern

Same frame in shade

White poles on
the framework of the
fence cast a strong
shadow.

Light-colored fence with
dark battens.
1″ x 12″ vertical siding.

Redwood left to weather.
Battens are used
as supports for climbing
roses.

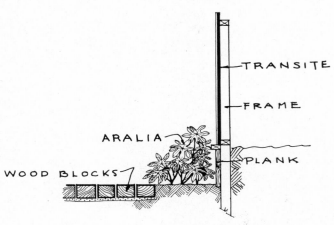

TRANSITE

FRAME

ARALIA

WOOD BLOCKS

PLANK

CORRUGATED ASBESTOS

Corrugated or plain asbestos (transite) is an excellent fence material. It can be sawed, nailed, and painted and is fireproof and decay-proof. It comes in 42-inch widths and in several lengths.

It relies for decorative interest not only on its own structure but on alternating patterns of sun and shade. Since shadow knows no season, this motif becomes a dominant design element in the garden in both winter and summer.

◀ REAR VIEW

BOLTED TO
A PIPE FRAME

BOARD AND BATTEN

Of all the fences handed down to us from previous eras, the board and batten fence still holds its own.

Practical and neat, it looks well in most gardens and with most simple houses.

It can create a variety of effects, depending upon the size of the lumber used and the kind of finish. It may be built of rough lumber and left to weather, of resawn lumber and stained, or of surfaced wood and painted.

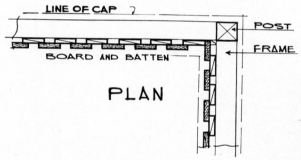

This variation of the board and batten fence has 1″ x 6″ resawn redwood boards pre-stained black, with 1″ x 4″ grey battens and white cap. The house is painted grey and white.

Were it not for the shameful freedom given to animals in the village streets, fences might be much lower and more open than now. *"Suburban Home Grounds"—F. J. Scott, 1870*

OPEN FENCES

Open sections of fence are invaluable when you
want a sense of enclosure but still want to
see through to greenery or a view. Fences inside
the garden can use this idea to make the
ending seem less abrupt.

A LOUVERED FENCE

This louvered fence, which screens the cut flower garden from the terrace, does not interrupt the continuity of the view or of the prevailing breeze.

CHAMBERLAIN GARDEN 1948

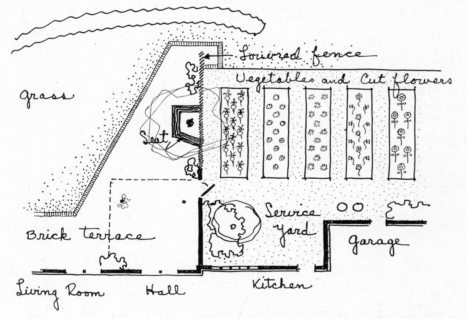

Awake, O, North Wind and come thou South; blow upon my garden that the spices thereof may flow out. *"Song of Solomon"*

195

Grewia caffra is trained in 30-inch squares on the wall of a two-story house.

Grapevines on a white wall

PLANT PATTERNS
ON WALLS

The use of plants on vertical surfaces is not new, but takes on added significance as our gardens get smaller and more enclosed.

Our tendency to find more and more uses for the flat areas (other than for plants) has led us to look inquiringly at vertical surfaces as possible additional garden space.

If the orientation is suitable for them, vines, fruit trees, and ornamentals can be espaliered naturally or in pattern on any house wall or fence.

They may be used to reduce glare, to cast shadows, to absorb noise, to raise fruit, to grow flowers, to enrich the design, and in some cases to *be* the design.

A formal boxwood garden is screened from the street by an eight-foot wood fence, with variegated ivy in a diamond pattern.

Ivy on brick

Paving

Paving—something hard and convenient under
foot—has been man's concern ever since
he came down out of the trees.

Paving to keep his feet dry—paving to pull his
chariots over—paving to accommodate
mobs of people—paving to walk on in a garden.

The cobblestones of Europe represent centuries of
labor by men determined to pull themselves
out of the mud of the Middle Ages.
Their patterns, from the bold cobblestones of the
Paris streets to the pebble mosaics of Spain,
have been an inspiration to all garden designers.

VILLA D'ESTE

STOCKHOLM

FIFTH AVENUE

200

PAVING

MAKES YEAR-ROUND PATTERN

Paving is one of the major design elements in the garden. Different materials
may be combined in an infinite variety of patterns to satisfy the designer
and intrigue the observer.

Paving is not necessarily just a terrace plus a network of paths leading to
various parts of the garden. It may cover large areas and hold within
itself plots of grass and flowers, trees, rock outcroppings, and pools.

Paving cannot substitute for the expanse of open lawn on a large property, but
the relative proportion of paving to grass can often be increased with
good results. In hot or subtropical climates, large paved areas will radiate too
much heat unless shaded; but for the average house on a small lot
the amount of paving can be greatly increased without robbing us of the
fundamental pleasures of a garden.

Paving must be sympathetic with the grass, trees, and flowers upon whose
domain it has encroached and must set them off to their best advantage.
They will in turn enhance the paving by softening its outlines and casting their
shadows across it.

Paving leaves less area for planting, but since there are fewer plants, they should
be selected with more care and cared for with more enthusiasm.

If complicated paving patterns and colors
are introduced into an already exciting composition, the resulting confusion,
rivaling Joseph's coat, may be a
constant irritation.

It may be the role of paving to remain calm
—to be the common denominator
and a foil for the excitement created by
fences, steps, grass forms, brilliant
flower combinations, foliage textures, and
distant views.

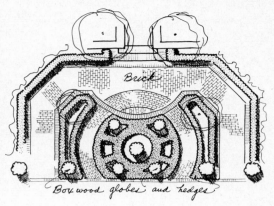

An entrance garden with brick weaving a pattern in the paving.

A parterre of boxwood gives permanent green, enlivened by seasonal color.

Concrete bands, brick, and petunias give interest and color in an otherwise green garden.

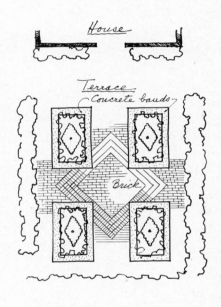

THESE THREE GARDENS are mainly green—all in places where a year-round, well-groomed look is preferred. The main color and interest are provided by the pattern and texture of the paving materials. In each case, seasonal color adds to the picture, but the planting is permanent and green throughout the year.

Bricks set in mortar make a border for flagstone laid with open joints and planted with woolly thyme, camomile, dwarf pinks, and alpines.

WOOD

Wood is a sympathetic material; it is warm,
friendly, and unobtrusive, having neither
the weight nor the visual importance of masonry.

It can be recommended for paving once you
accept its shortcomings—its tendency to decay and
to become slippery in shady places.

Squares of heartwood (these are railroad ties, creo-
soted) last much longer than round sections of logs (which have a sap ring), but neither
should be considered as permanent until a
satisfactory preservative is developed.

Washed aggregate with 2 x 4 redwood dividers

Tan concrete—broom finish

CONCRETE

Ordinarily the plain troweled concrete of our city sidewalks is not an attractive garden paving.

But with a little more effort and expense, concrete can become both useful and attractive when color, texture, and pattern are added.

Almost any color is obtainable in preparations to be either mixed with the concrete or applied afterwards. Earth colors are the safest—buff, tan, brown, and warm greys. (Greens and blues tend to fade and compete with foliage colors.)

Variations in texture can be obtained by brooming the surface or exposing the aggregate.

Bands of wood, brick, tile, or mosaic pebbles can be introduced for added interest and for pattern. They automatically provide expansion joints.

WASHED CONCRETE OR
EXPOSED AGGREGATE

1.

2.

Illustrated here are several steps in the installation of exposed aggregate paving.

1. The header boards are installed—complete with spikes to key the wood to the concrete.

2. Local conditions warranted the use of base rock under this slab. Grate covering of catch-basin is carefully set to relate to the pattern.

3. Cement finishers are hosing concrete and carefully brooming it to remove cement film without loosening top aggregate. The texture may be varied, depending on the size of aggregate used and the amount of brooming.

You must conſtantly obſerve to lay your terraſſes with a small inſenſible declivity for carrying off the water as an inch or half an inch in a fathom. *"The Theory and Practice of Gardening"—Alexander Le Blond 1728*

3.

Seats

GARDENS ARE MADE TO SIT IN

There's nothing more inviting than large comfortable furniture on a large comfortable terrace.

But there's a limit to storage space and a limit to one's patience when too many chairs have to be moved in out of the rain. Permanently-built seats can accommodate large groups in a garden with a minimum amount of movable furniture. Visually the seats become part of the over-all design, cutting sharp shadows and creating strong patterns.

Although the most comfortable width is eighteen inches, they may be as wide as thirty inches, so people can sit on either side, or use them as buffet or cocktail tables.

They may be open underneath, where a feeling of lightness is desired, or when the line of vision should not be stopped and especially when paving or grass continue beyond the seat.

They may be free-standing or retain a tree, a house wall, or a slope.

A narrow retaining wall may become a useful garden feature by the addition of a cap wide enough to sit on, and besides, the added width is pleasanter to look at.

A seat wall retains a flower border.

Build a seat along a sunny house wall where there is reflected heat and protection from the wind. It will hold a half dozen people who can't all get chairs in the sun.

One end of this seat is wide enough for a serving table.

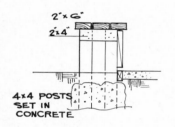

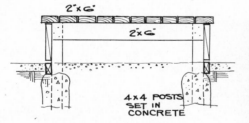

Solid seating in and around a terrace, wide enough for sunbathing or a buffet.

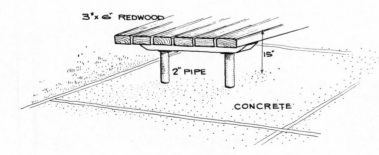

Open seat on pipe legs made of 3″ x 6″; the extra thickness allows a longer span between supports.

207

Curbs

BRADLEY GARDEN, HILLSBOROUGH

Around the outside walls ran flower beds raised one to two feet above the ground by bricks or plants. . . . The paths, usually sanded, were bordered by flowers held in place with stones or animal bones or tiles. *"The Story of Gardening— Richardson Wright, 1938 (describing mediaeval gardens)*

VEGETABLE GARDEN

FLOWER BORDER

Walls of concrete and wood separated by a flower border.

RAISED PLANTING BEDS

Curbs may be low and simply define a planting space or they may be higher and broader and comfortable to sit on. They may be used in a flower or vegetable garden to create raised beds at a convenient working height.

When a retaining wall is too high, you can build a lower one in front of it and leave a strip between for planting. The space may be for only a few flowers or it may be wide enough for planting to screen or soften the higher wall.

Raising this flower border reduces the apparent height of the fence and creates a strong shadow as a base line for the color.

TURNER GARDEN, MODESTO 1942

magnolia
Hedge
Fence
Ivy
BRICK

To gain height on a flat lot, a brick wall (seat high) was built 10 feet inside the property line. The planting space was raised with excess earth from the site.

To insure privacy a fence was built for a screen, a hedge planted to absorb noise, and magnolias added to plant out nearby second-story windows.

DOUBLE WALLS
WERE THE SOLUTION FOR THIS GARDEN

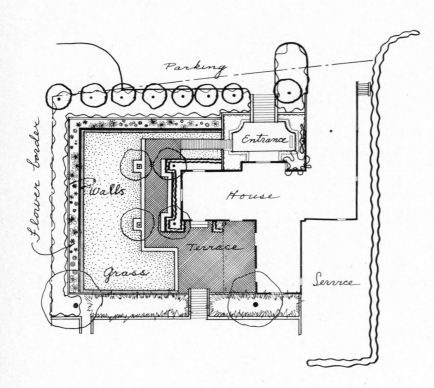

When the bulldozer finished grading the McAllisters' lot there was a cut six feet high on two sides.

They wanted an extensive flower border and not a six-foot retaining wall, so they built two walls and put the flowers between them. The space gave Martha McAllister a raised bed 120 feet long in which to garden, which suited her perfectly, as she is an expert on flower borders. It is four feet wide; she says it should have been six so she could arrange the flowers more effectively, and she's right.

The low wall is two feet high; the back wall, four feet. Above them is the planting which screens the garden from the road.

Brick is laid in a straight herringbone pattern. The 18-inch border of concrete has a coarse sand finish.

Pink-flowering horsechestnuts shade the terrace.

PARIS

CURBS KEEP A GARDEN NEAT

The greatest value of curbs around planting beds is their ability to contain a design which might otherwise become obliterated by time and planting. The pattern will be retained even if the beds are unplanted.

If a softer effect is desired, use low hedges or borders.

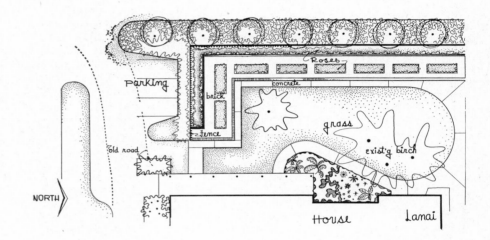

Between the house and the street was once an open front lawn, but Agnes Crocket wanted more privacy, more parking, and a rose garden. She wanted it all very, very neat.

Now a board and batten fence keeps the garden private. The driveway was widened to get parking for three cars. The balance is for roses and grass.

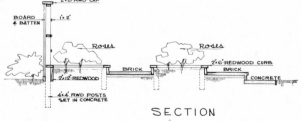

SECTION

This is the winter effect with the roses mulched. Flowering pears (Pyrus Kawakami) are espaliered on the fence.

The rose garden

is set on a brick platform 6 inches high, and the rose beds are raised another 6 inches in redwood curbs.

Here curbs provide crispness and shadow and keep the garden looking neat and well tended.

In the Crocket garden they are of wood, but they could be built of brick, stone, or any other desirable material.

Raising this part of the garden has resulted in additional interest on an otherwise flat lot; it was done primarily to provide 12 inches of topsoil for the roses in an area of heavy soil and poor drainage.

MR. & MRS. HOWARD HICKINGBOTHAM, HILLSBOROUGH 1948

The Seventh Fleet in action.

It's your turn to come and see *us*.

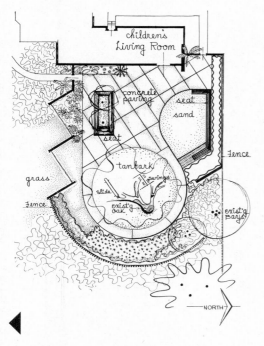

The wing added to the house includes a playroom which
opens onto an area with a sunny
sandbox and a tree for
shade.

The fence screens the play yard
from the street.

WHICH WILL SURVIVE,

THE CHILDREN OR THE GARDEN?

A young couple, building a house and planning to raise a family
and to have a garden as well, should take certain precau-
tions to insure the garden's survival as well as to provide freedom for the children to play. It's no fun if
you're constantly slapping their hands.

Those who plan a small playground set apart from adult activities and expect the children to stay there happily for
hours underestimate the average child's desire to be right where
you are. Organized play space and equipment are fine, but
there are many days when they will prefer to be up in a tree,
or in an old crate in the next lot, or behind a machine
gun in the bottom of your sweet pea trench.

Play space with plenty of equipment, starting with a sand pile
and continuing through swings, rings, and slides to
basketball standards, will generally keep a family of children well
contented. But if you intend to have a garden at the same
time, it is wise to arrange the path system so that bicycles won't
be tempted to cut corners, and to provide raised
curbs along your favorite flower beds.

Children get tired of going back and forth; they like to go
around. Plan it that way—so they have a hazard course around
benches and trees with plenty of leeway on the curves.
To turn a tricycle on a three-foot walk, especially if it has several wagons in tow, can ruin a whole bed of tulips.
It's all a matter of planning. Life can be beautiful for a family
of six children—and so can the garden.

THE SHAPE OF THE POOL

Site restrictions and your reason for wanting a pool will influence its size and shape.

If you are a veteran swimmer and do twenty laps before breakfast, you should have a rectangular pool with straight ends. Length should be favored over width. How long it will be depends on your property and your pocketbook.

If the pool is to be used mainly by children and average swimmers or as a center for social activity, you may select any shape you like.

When it fits your needs, there's no reason not to use one of the standard shapes offered by the pool companies. The simplest is the rectangle with rounded corners. The classic shapes are best in more formal settings.

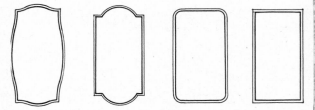

If a standard pool will not fit into the available space with proper orientation and sufficient room for terrace and pool activities, furniture and planting, then one must be designed to fit the area. There is not too much penalty cost-wise. There are many interesting variations. These forms produce more shallow area for children:

This one increases both the shallow and deep water areas:

These fit into odd-shaped lots:

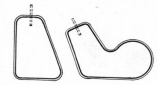

This pool fits into a preconceived architectural pattern:

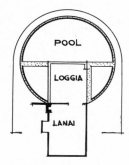

DONNELL GARDEN, SONOMA

HANISCH GARDEN, PASADENA

Swimming pools

HICKINGBOTHAM GARDEN, HILLSBOROUGH

THE PRIVATE SWIMMING POOL, ONCE A LUXURY FOR THE FEW, SEEMS TO BE HERE TO STAY FOR THE MANY

Pooles marre all, and make the garden un-
wholsome and full of Flies, and Frogs.
"Of Gardens"—Francis Bacon, 1561–1626

The pool is a place to gather around, much as a fireplace is in a room. It offers swimming for the athlete, or just getting wet if you're hot. If you don't even want to watch, there is large comfortable furniture for sun-bathing, sleeping, or relaxing.

It can remain a simple reflection pool in the garden, in which you occasionally take a dip, or become a complete entertainment center where you have as many fascinations for children and guests as you can dream up. It may have a cabana with shade and lemonade, or maybe it has a bar. If there are youngsters around, it might have a soda fountain and a sandwich counter. If your guests stay for the week end, it can double as a guest house.

If you think you will want a pool some time (when the children are a little older or when you can afford it), let it be a part of your master plan now, so you won't put large, immovable objects where the pool should be. Think of the grades, the orientation for sun and shade and protection from wind. Think of access for the pool contractor, who would like to bring a loader and trucks right to the pool area.

Also, think very seriously about having just a quiet garden, particularly if grandmother has built a pool to lure the children to her house. A pool is fun, but it is also an expense and a responsibility.

When you're told you can have a pool for from $3,000 to $5,000, get out your pencil. If you can slip a pool easily and without confusion into your lawn and not have to add another thing, you're lucky.

The case history of the average pool owner is different. After one month of children in wet bathing suits in the house, you will be convinced that something *must* be built out by the pool. It can be simple—open-air dressing rooms behind fences or hedges— or it may develop into a full-fledged lanai with dressing rooms, toilets, showers, and a barbecue. If you are just building your house, have the architect plan for a bathroom with outside access; it will save trouble and expense later.

You will need some paved area around the pool for sun-bathing and furniture; the filter and heater must be housed, and some storage room for equipment and cushions is a sound idea.

The cost of what you need, plus the cost of putting the garden back together again, equals about double the original cost of the pool.

WEILL GARDEN, SARATOGA

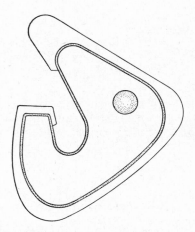

POOLS CAN BE MADE-TO-MEASURE

If you want a special pool to fit your property or your fancy, you will need one that's custom-designed.

You can have a pool which keeps the divers separate from the swimmers or the children away from both.

It can have a peninsula to sit on or an island to swim to. Broad steps and underwater seats can increase its use, and tile mosaics and sculpture may adorn it.

REGALDO GARDEN, SAN SALVADOR

A pool for adults and children with an island to swim to. The island will have a sunshade and cushions and all you will need is a floating tray to bring over the martinis.

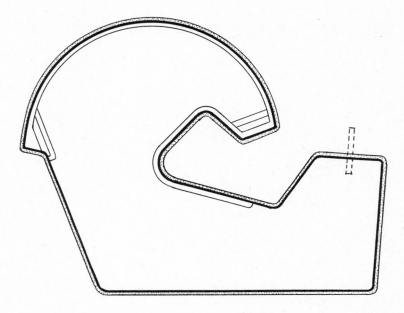

MOROSANI GARDEN, LITCHFIELD, CONNECTICUT

This pool has separate areas for swimming and diving, with ample shallow water for play where it doesn't interfere with swimming. It's designed to please everyone, from children and timid elderly ladies to Olympic champions.

The future terrace, with gaily-colored furniture and a sunshade, will seem to float in the pool.

MENUHIN GARDEN, ALMA 1942

MARTIN GARDEN, WOODSIDE 1954

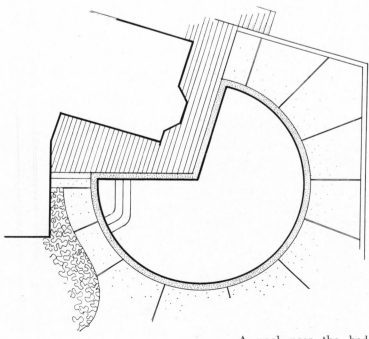

A pool near the bed-
rooms—its shape
influenced by a restricted
site.

BEFORE

AFTER

An established garden may need considerable reorganization to accommodate a swimming pool.

When the Phillipses decided to install a pool, the only logical place for it seemed to be in the garage turnaround, which was sunny and well related to the proposed new living room.

The original garage was remodeled to provide many of the things they wanted—a large storage room, a room and bath for the gardener, a small shop, a lanai and bar.

Dressing rooms were combined with the new carport.

The existing well-organized garden work area was not changed.

PHOTOGRAPHER: PIRKLE JONES

Marine designs, in black and white on a seagreen background, decorate the wall of the terrace which forms one side of the pool.

The glazed tile mural was designed and executed by Mary Erckenbrack of San Francisco.

DR. & MRS. HUGH DAVID PHILLIPS, ATHERTON 1954

ARCHITECT: LESLIE I. NICHOLS

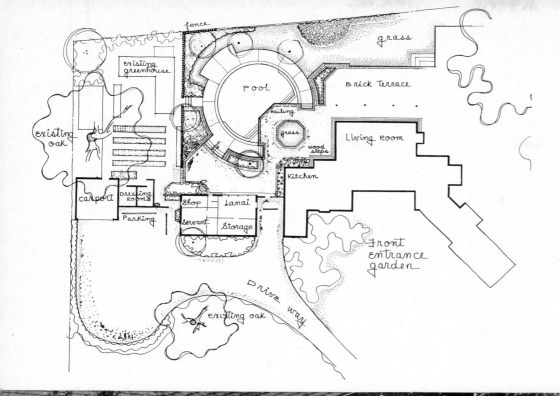

fence

grass

existing
greenhouse

pool

Brick Terrace

railing

existing
oak

grass

Living Room

wood
steps

Kitchen

carport

Dressing
Rooms

Shop

Lanai

Parking

Servant

Storage

Front
entrance
garden

Drive way

existing oak

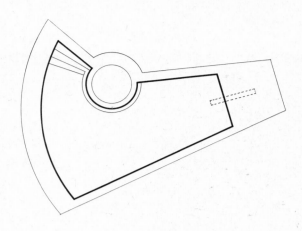

PLAY SPACE AND SWIMMERS

ARE SEPARATED

The Meins wanted a pool with 45 feet of uninterrupted swimming. They wanted plenty of shallow area for small children to play in and a convenient place near the pool to watch them.

The shape of their pool defines the swimming lanes and provides a peninsula large enough for a table and an umbrella. The children are close, and the view of the diving is excellent.

The children can play on the wide steps. The second step continues around the circle to make the underwater seat.

POOLHOUSE BY WURSTER, BERNARDI & EMMONS, ARCHITECTS

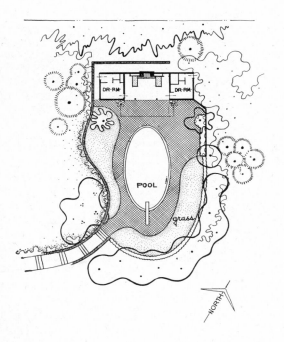

The Bradleys have a 25′ x 50′ oval pool located on the lowest of three terraces below the house.

They wanted a shelter which could be used as an outdoor room for relaxing and bridge and as a lanai for the pool, with dressing rooms which could also serve as overnight guest rooms.

Large glass doors slide back against the dressing room walls. When they are closed, the fireplace makes the room comfortable for entertaining on cool evenings.

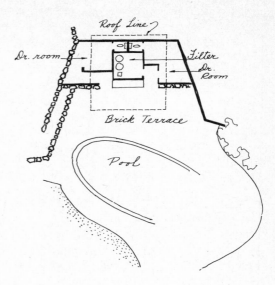

DUFF GARDEN, KENT WOODLANDS 1946

A grapestake fence conceals the
dressing rooms and filter
which are shaded by a light wooden
roof.

A SHELTER BY THE POOL
IS A CENTER FOR FAMILY LIVING

Whatever the structure at the pool is called—
cabana, pool house, lanai, or garden room
—it serves many purposes.

Space can be provided for dressing rooms, filter
and heating equipment, furniture storage,
cupboards for dishes and barbecue equipment, and
counters for serving. You can have electrical
outlets for a refrigerator, percolator, radio, and TV
and a jack for a telephone. There can be a
fireplace or a pit for an open campfire at night.

A pool house often adds that extra room the
house needs when teen-age entertaining
is more than it can cope with.

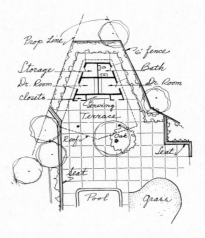

A flat wood roof floats over the terrace, dressing rooms, and
filter room. Closets on each side of
the serving counter holds
supplies, cushions and sun mattresses.

Raised flower beds keep the terrace
clean and provide extra
seating.

de ROOS GARDEN, SAN MATEO 1952

A wall, a roofed area, and minimum open dressing rooms terminate this view from the house terrace. Howard Hickingbotham is handy with tools and built it himself.

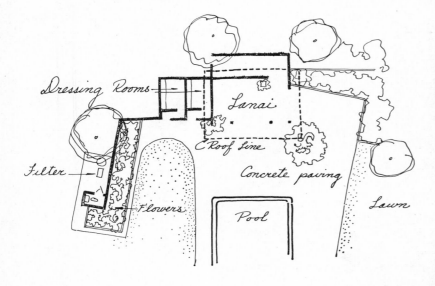

HICKINGBOTHAM GARDEN, HILLSBOROUGH 1948

227

MR. & MRS. ALFRED DUCATO, ATHERTON 1952   ARCHITECT FOR POOL HOUSE: GERMANO A. MILONO

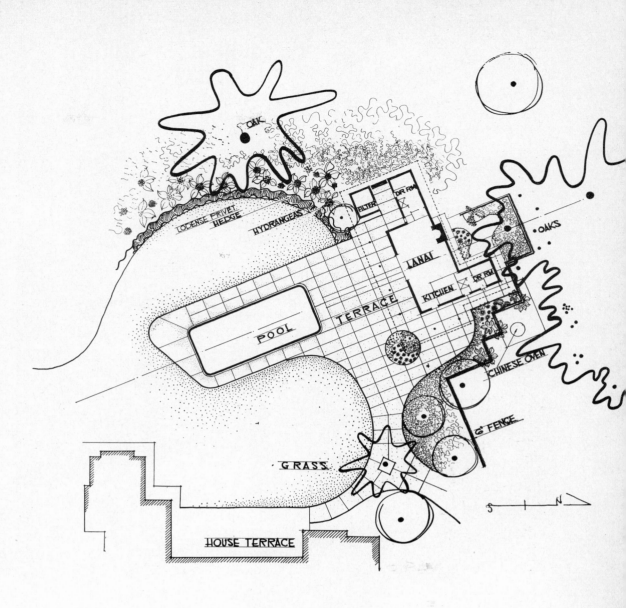

MORE ▶

Marie Ducato wanted more than just a shelter at her pool. She wanted to be able to stay out there all day if she felt like it and to entertain easily for lunch, bridge, garden club meetings, or cocktails.

The lounge, comfortably furnished and with a fireplace, can be closed on cool evenings. There is a bar and a small but complete kitchen which can provide anything from a snack to a full meal.

LANDSCAPE CONTRACTOR: OUTDOOR CONSTRUCTION, INC.

PHOTOGRAPHER: MAYNARD PARKER
POOL BY LANDON POOLS INC.

A small enclosed garden
behind the lanai,
with ferns and hydran-
geas, can be seen
from the pool terrace.

A view from the pool house showing the wide expanse of terrace
when the sliding sash are open.

Under the eaves are Hawaiian tree ferns in boxes, which are win-
tered in the greenhouse. Aralia Sieboldi, with its handsome large leaves, is used in profusion.

A Lodense privet hedge makes a crisp border for the hydrangea
planting.

Paving is white concrete, with redwood dividers stained black.

There's an
outside shower in one
corner.
Hawaiian torches
are used to light the garden at night.

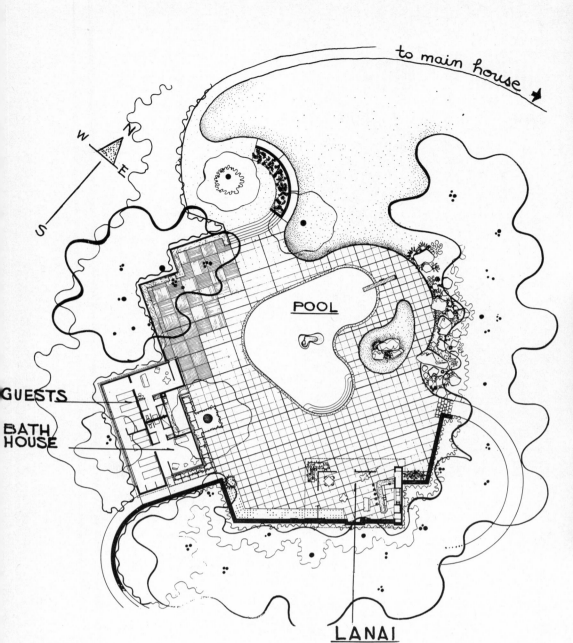

to main house →

POOL

GUESTS

BATH
HOUSE

LANAI

A FREE-FORM POOL IS AT HOME
IN THIS NATURAL SETTING

Built on a knoll on the Donnell Ranch, this pool and recreation area take advantage of a frame of live oaks offering wind protection and shade, native boulders, and a thirty-mile panoramic view of the San Francisco Bay area.

The pool, its shape inspired by the winding creeks of the salt marshes below, was designed to provide adequate space for all water activities. It has a shallow area for children near the recreation room, 60 feet of unobstructed swimming, and a deep section for diving.

The concrete terrace around the pool is colored tan to reduce glare. Three people are not lost on it nor are a hundred crowded.

MORE ▶

THE SCULPTURED ISLAND

The first idea was to use one of the big boulders from the site as a play island in the pool. This was changed (the rough rock would have torn the swimmers to pieces) into an island of concrete designed by sculptor Adaline Kent.

It separates the swimming and play areas and is a center of fun for divers and underwater experts who swim through a hole in the base.

Like most islands these days, it's crowded with sun-bathers.

The bathhouse faces the view and is land-scaped by the shadow of a tree.

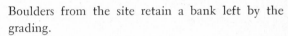

Boulders from the site retain a bank left by the grading.

The pool house at the Donnells has two sides of glass to take advantage of the view. When the sliding doors are open, the lanai becomes a part of the terrace, and the long bench follows the stone wall into the room to the fireplace. By sliding the side glass door into a slot in the stone wall, the room may be closed and heated.

There are complete facilities for entertainment, including a fully-equipped soda fountain for the children.

The bench is 4 feet 6 inches wide and
13 inches high, with the top hinged
so it can be used for storage. Cushions of
foam rubber cover it in the summer.

ASSOCIATE ARCHITECTS: GEORGE T. ROCKRISE AND GERMANO MILONO
CONSTRUCTION: W. S. BICKFORD   PHOTOGRAPHER: RONDAL PARTRIDGE

Garden work areas and service yards

Every garden should have a place to pot a plant, to store the fertilizers, to hang up the tools, and to build a compost pit. It may vary in size from a workbench and closet to an efficient gardening center.

Ready-made greenhouses, cold frames, lath houses, and storage walls may be combined to make any desired arrangement.

A service yard can include many things, but storage for gardening equipment and tools and the overflow from the house seems to be what people need most. The area becomes a small "corporation yard" for the things you won't throw away—that small stack of 2 x 4's, the pile of second-hand brick, the cartons of coke bottles, and the half-dead Christmas azalea, which must go somewhere until something can be done about them. There should be room for storing wood where it will be dry and a place for airing the woolens.

The gardening and house service units may be combined or completely separated, whichever works better.

Steps will be saved if these areas are near the center of activity and can be conveniently reached by a pick-up truck or at least a wheelbarrow.

Services areas are as important to the functioning of a garden as the kitchen is to the house and should always be included in the over-all planning.

GRUNSKY—BEFORE

GRUNSKY GARDEN,
STOCKTON

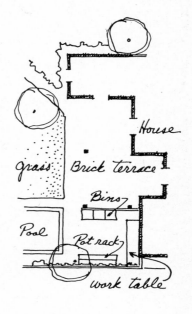

Your work area need not be hidden from sight or relegated to leftover and often inconvenient spots.

The MacBrides extended their brick terrace and built a simple unit with soil bins, work space, and pot racks.

Cooking has come out onto the terrace, so why not gardening?

MACBRIDE GARDEN, MODESTO 1947

WEST GARDEN, STOCKTON 1947

ITALY, 1952

Mowing Strips are narrow bands of hard paving, level with, and at the edge of, a lawn. They provide a track for one wheel of the mower, minimize hand-trimming and keep the grass shape intact and free from encroaching plants.

They provide a decorative, permanent border and strengthen the garden pattern where a crisp neat line is desired.

A COMPLETE SERVICE AREA FOR A SMALL GARDEN

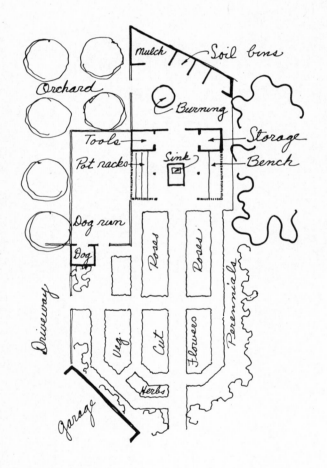

Most of the things a gardener could want are in this work unit.

The owner can raise his own vegetables and cut flowers and arrange them at the center table, where there's a sink and storage space for vases and equipment.

On one side of the arbor is a potting bench with soil bins underneath and on the other side are racks for potted plants.

Twin storage rooms contain all necessary garden tools and supplies.

MR. & MRS. MERRITT SPEIDEL, PALO ALTO

The Dana deHarts' demands were simple and direct—a garden easy to look at and easy to care for.

They wanted simple planting, with perhaps just a few each of their favorite things—camellias, tree ferns, rhododendrons, fuchsias, and hydrangeas. They wanted lots of ivy, and a terrace out under the large live oak tree at the bottom of the garden.

Except for their favorite plants, the house sits in a sea of ivy which reaches to the property lines, broken only by the curving asphalt paths. The simplicity of the planting gives the garden a serenity seldom found except in gardens of great age.

The deHarts' oak tree was at the bottom of the garden, and under it was to be a terrace. But the day the house was finished a wind tipped the tree over toward the house.

While this seemed a catastrophe when it happened, they discovered it would live and that it was now near the house—a better location for their terrace.

Metal posts were added to keep the tree from settling further, and when the foliage was cleared, it became a natural bower. The terrace—a redwood deck—is under it, a seat on light metal supports is in its shade, and baskets of fuchsias hang from its branches.

Before the oak fell   *and after*

In the place where the tree falleth,
there it shall be. *"Ecclesiastes," XI-3*

MORE ▶

MR. & MRS. DANA C. deHART, HILLSBOROUGH 1953

DEHART GARDEN

I never had any other de-
sire so strong, and so like to
Covetousness, as . . . that
I might be master at last of
a small house and large
Garden, with very moder-
ate conveniences joined to
them. . . . *"The Garden"*
—Abraham Cowley (1618–
1667)

This is the last garden on the tour. It was saved until last because it's the story of a tree and because it's the story about people who knew just what they wanted their garden to do for them and are happy in it.

It isn't a garden that everyone would want or should have. For instance, it wouldn't do for a family with growing children, for there's no grass to play on.

It wouldn't do for people who entertain lavishly, for there's no swimming pool, no lanai, no barbecue.

It wouldn't do for someone who gardens intensely, for it's too shady for many flowers, too small for sweeping borders, and too relaxed for potting benches, asparagus beds, and power mowers.

But for the DeHarts, who like their sea of ivy, their terrace under the live oak, and their hanging baskets, it's just right.

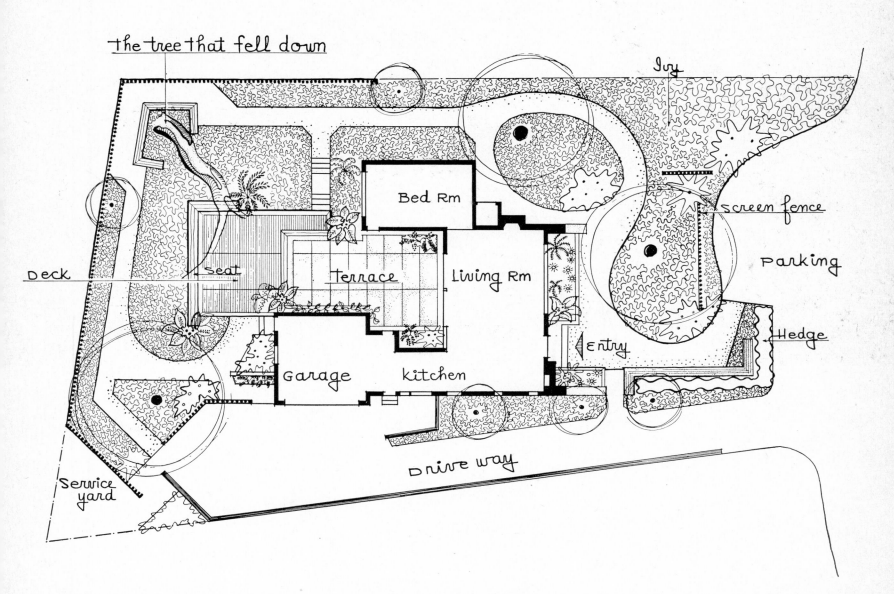

You've come to the end of the tour.

If it seemed too brief, remember we had a lot of ground to cover.

If it was too long, I hope you stopped to rest.

If I've talked too much, I can only quote from Cato, who said in a letter to a friend, "Had I more time, I would have written you a shorter letter."

What you will have, I hope, is a garden more beautiful than you had anticipated, with less care than you had expected, and costing only a little more than you had planned.

INDEX